BEYOND THE
WEST HORIZON

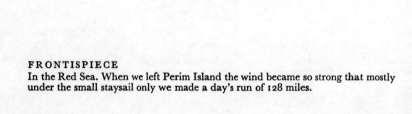

FRONTISPIECE
In the Red Sea. When we left Perim Island the wind became so strong that mostly under the small staysail only we made a day's run of 128 miles.

BEYOND THE WEST HORIZON

ERIC C. HISCOCK

Author of
Wandering Under Sail
Cruising Under Sail
Around the World in Wanderer III
Voyaging Under Sail
Atlantic Cruise in Wanderer III
Sou'West in Wanderer IV
Come Aboard

WITH 46 PHOTOGRAPHS
BY THE AUTHOR AND HIS WIFE
AND 9 CHARTS

SHERIDAN HOUSE

Published in the United States of America 1987 by
Sheridan House Inc., 145 Palisade St, Dobbs Ferry,
New York 10522

First published in Great Britain
in hardback by Oxford University Press 1963
Published in paperback by Adlard Coles Ltd 1987
8 Grafton Street, London W1X 3LA

Copyright © Eric Hiscock 1963

ISBN 0-911378-71-5

Printed and bound in Great Britain

For

SUSAN

*without whose cheerful encouragement
and co-operation this voyage could
never have been brought to a
successful conclusion*

Acknowledgement

The acknowledgements of the author are due to the Editors of *Yachting* and *Yachting World*, in which magazines some parts of this story were first published.

Contents

Illustrations

Charts

Plans

The plans of *Wanderer III* are reproduced by kind permission
of her designers, Laurent Giles & Partners, Ltd., of Lymington,
Hampshire, to whom the author and publisher express thanks
for their co-operation.

1

A Second Voyage, and Why

Some years ago Susan, my wife, and I sailed our 30-ft. yacht *Wanderer III** round the world, a three-year trip which gave us great pleasure, some excitement, and a satisfying feeling of achievement. On our return home we were surprised by the interest that was shown in the voyage, and much to our astonishment found ourselves largely engaged for four winters travelling the country and giving illustrated talks. These lecture tours took us to many places of which we had never previously heard. Our audiences totalled something over 60,000. Few members of them were directly interested in the sea, and some had never even seen it; but they came, I think, because our theme was travel by an unusual means to places which are not easy of access; we were not hard-case seamen, but a normal (we hope) married couple, so they could put themselves in imagination in our place, and perhaps one day do what we had done. Our pictures were not the blue and white flicker of the television screen, but in colour which was startling in its beauty on a dark, wet, winter evening in a drab manufacturing town. Above all, we had been *round the world*, and there is magic in those words.

The excitement of facing a new audience each night, unable to judge in advance what its reaction is likely to be, and the pleasure to be had if by its laughter, its silence in the right places, and its applause, it showed appreciation, made this for us a rewarding occupation.

But often as we travelled on the ferry between the mainland

* See Appendix 1, page 187.

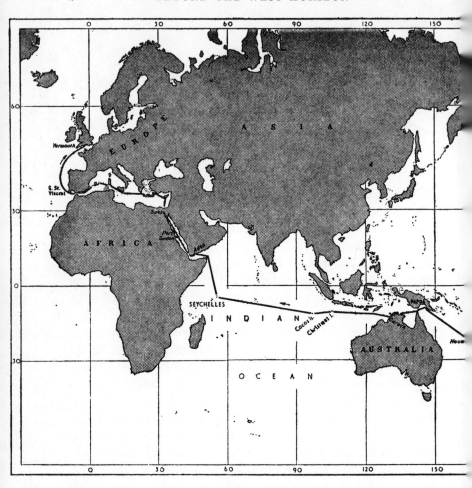

THE TRACK OF *WANDERER III* ON HER SECON·

and the Isle of Wight, where we live, we looked out through
Hurst Narrows and beyond the Needles lighthouse to the western
horizon, knowing that we had only to slip out through those
narrows in *Wanderer III* and keep going in a south-westerly
direction to reach in time the area where the warm trade winds
blow; they would carry us on over the blue and rolling sea
until one day a landfall with a strange-sounding name—perhaps some colourful island with gleaming beaches, leaning

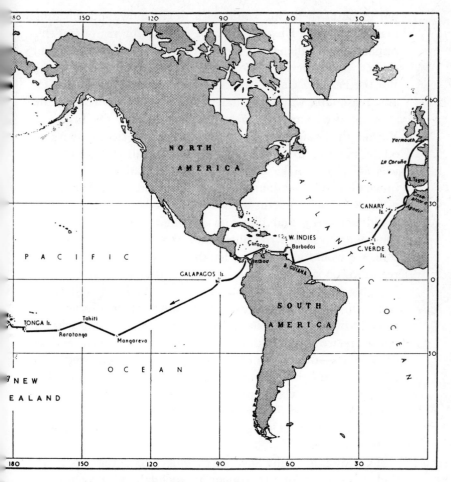

CIRCUMNAVIGATION OF THE WORLD

palms, and haunting music (here our thoughts dwelt particularly on the South Pacific)—lifted out of the sea ahead. The
salt water that washes the shores of the Isle of Wight could also
break on the barrier reef of Tahiti.

On our earlier voyage we had made a chain of friends around
the world; what a pleasure it would be for us to visit them again,
and what a surprise for them! But we must not keep too closely
to our earlier track; there were many, many places we could

not touch at then, but would wish to visit now, and this time, maybe, we would have to accept (chiefly for reasons of self-respect) the challenge of the Red Sea, instead of taking the earlier, and easier, way home round the Cape of Good Hope. But the Panama Canal would have to see us again, as it is the only reasonable way for a small sailing vessel to reach the Pacific.

A hundred yards or so up the creek above the bridge at Yarmouth *Wanderer* lay idly, and perhaps impatiently, swinging on her mooring to the tide, and although a fair amount of work was needed to make her in all respects ready for sea again, much of it could be done with our own hands. It should not be difficult to find a tenant to look after our house and garden. I could not write and illustrate any more books until I had something fresh to write about and photograph (this time, we said, we would also try our hands at movie making and tape recording),* and the books I had written were at the time bringing in royalties enough at least to enable us to start the trip, after which I must earn by writing articles. Indeed, we thought of every possible reason and excuse for doing what in our hearts we longed to do. The difficulties, the dangers, and the discomforts—the problems of pilotage among coral reefs, the handling of the ship in bad weather, the long, dark nights when it hurts to keep awake and steer a careful compass course, the heat, the flies, the mosquitoes, and the officials of the ports—seemed just then of no great importance. In short, we were getting itchy feet.

That disease might have taken longer to develop properly had it not been for the women of Rochdale. Our agents had engaged us to give a show to the Rochdale Women's Luncheon Club in the town hall. For the past ten days we had been travelling in the Midlands and the North, giving one and sometimes two shows a day, so perhaps we were a little jaded and easily upset; but it did seem thoughtless of the Rochdale

* See Appendix 2, page 193.

PLATE I
Wanderer III. For her second circumnavigation we gave our 30 ft. sloop working sails of tan-dyed terylene, and a black and gold globe as a figurehead.

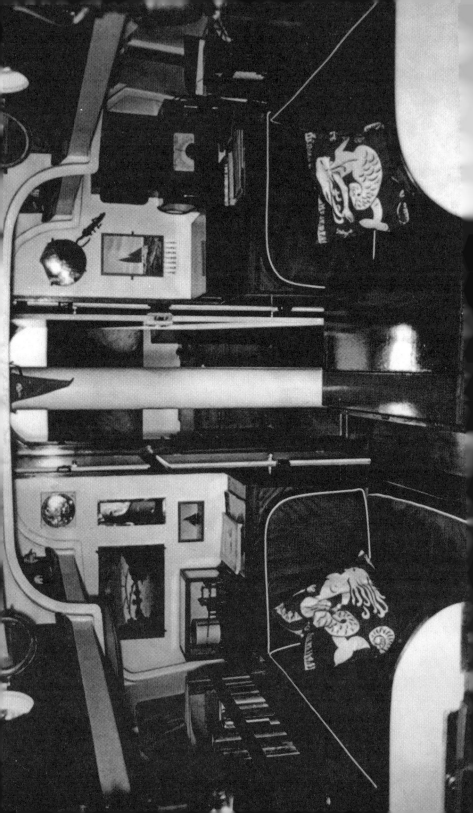

ladies to have failed to black out the room in which we were to show our slides, particularly as the screen had been placed between two bright and inaccessible windows (the curtains, they said, had been sent away to be cleaned), and in loud voices to discuss one another's hats throughout the talk.

That evening we had to change trains at Todmorden railway station, and while we waited we discussed the women of Rochdale, the children in Burnley library (who throw things), and the Rothwell Teachers and Parents Association (who fidget and rattle coffee-cups), forgetting for the moment our wonderful reception in the Caird Hall, Dundee, where they turned out 1,800 strong and applauded every slide, and the grand affair in Church House, Westminster, to which a distinguished and appreciative company came.

For a little while there was silence between us, and I wondered idly what new discomforts our hotel would produce that night. A fire burned red in the huge bogie stove, the smoke-grimed posters looked yellow in the light from a single hissing gas mantle; our fellow travellers stamped their feet on the dirty floor and whistled tunelessly, and from the foggy night outside came the mournful hoot of a locomotive and the clatter of shunting goods wagons.

'Well,' said Susan presently, 'I think we ought to make another voyage in *Wanderer* while we can. There's really nothing to stop us.'

Wanderer III was then seven years old and had taken us in safety, if in no great comfort, some 40,000 miles. She was in good condition (we pride ourselves on keeping her that way), but the copper with which her bottom was sheathed as a protection against attack by worm had, through wastage in warm tropical waters, grown very thin; so we had it replaced with copper of heavier gauge, and the old copper was sold for what

---

PLATE 2
The cabin, which was our home for the three-year voyage, is about 8 ft. square. A few of our more highly prized possessions adorn the bulkheads: a pearl shell from Tahiti and a baby alligator from British Guiana to starboard, a Thurburn painting of the Helford River and the Blue Water Medal of America to port.

it had cost to remove to a fun fair for use on the dodg'em car floor, where it is needed to make electric contact. She had a 4 h.p. Stuart Turner two-stroke auxiliary engine, but although this was reliable it was of insufficient power for a vessel with considerable windage and a displacement of 9 tons; we had therefore failed to call at a number of interesting places on our earlier voyage because the engine could not drive the yacht against a moderate headwind, or a 3-knot current, in passes or channels too narrow or awkward to beat through under sail. So we had this replaced by a similar engine of 8 h.p., but as we did not increase the petrol capacity, the range under power in quiet conditions with no current was only about 80 miles. However, *Wanderer* is essentially a sailing vessel, and for the greater part of the voyage stores and water would be of more importance than fuel.

The sails (there are nine of them) were in fair condition, but we thought it wise to replace the old cotton mainsail and large staysail, and after some discussion with Cranfield & Carter, our sailmakers, we decided to have them made of terylene. This material, which had been in use among racing yachts for some time, has the advantage that when wet it does not get appreciably heavier or change shape; because it is stronger a lighter cloth can be used, and it is not seriously attacked by mildew. But at that time not much experience had been had with it on long ocean passages, and it was thought that the proud-standing stitches might chafe too readily; so we had each seam of the mainsail reinforced with a row of hand-stitching. In the event chafe did not prove to be a very serious problem, but the hand-stitching unfortunately puckered the sail, doing it no harm but giving it a rather odd appearance.

We also gave our ship a small vanity to wear on special occasions, a figurehead in the form of a globe with the sea in black and the land in gold leaf; this was made for us by David and Jean Cobb, the artists. (Since our return David has painted a lovely picture of *Wanderer* running in the north-east trade wind.)

With these important matters seen to, Susan and I set to work on the refit. We examined every item of gear and equipment, but found little that needed replacement; then with paint, varnish, and enamel we coated the ship from truck to waterline so that she gleamed. After that was done we moved her down into the main harbour, where we secured her fore-and-aft between two posts, and set about the business of storing and provisioning.

For Susan and me this is the most exciting part of the preparation for a voyage. As it is the last of all the jobs, we realize with a sudden quickening of the pulse and a curiously hollow feeling in the solar plexus that the time for departure is approaching, and the cosy days of preparation in a smooth, safe harbour are nearly done. As we stowed away the cases of tinned food, the items for the medicine chest and first-aid box, the cartons of films and tapes, the tropical clothes, the spare parts for engine, w.c., galley stove, lamps, and winches, the tins of paint, the shackles and blocks and the coils of rope and wire, and the hundred and one other things on the list, we wondered in what circumstances they would next come to light—at sea many miles from land, perhaps; in some warm and far-away place, or in some grave emergency; and we doubled our mental efforts to make sure that nothing vital had been forgotten, for although the world is not a desert, there are many places where some things are unobtainable; while at sea, of course, anything forgotten has to be done without, or a substitute improvised. And as the lockers and tanks and all hidden spaces got filled, but with room left for the last-minute stores—the greased eggs, the butter, the fruit and vegetables, the bread —the ship sat lower and still lower in the water; indeed, in full ocean-going trim she floated 9 in. below her designed water-line, but it must be said that this is not entirely due to the many things we put aboard, but to the fact that she was rather more heavily constructed than Jack Giles, her designer, originally intended.

At Yarmouth, where everyone takes a healthy interest in the affairs of his neighbours, it is not possible to prepare for a voyage without being quickly found out, and every time we landed at the quay, went to the shops, or visited other yachts, someone was almost sure to ask us when we were leaving or where we were going. We were ready to leave by mid-July, but as we had no desire to beat down Channel, we were not prepared to state a date in advance in case it dawned with a headwind. The second question was more difficult to deal with, for if we did not mention a destination it was assumed that we would just wander about wherever the winds chanced to blow us, which is contrary to our principles, for we contend that a successful voyage is a planned voyage, and that the greater the care taken in planning the more pleasurable and successful is the voyage likely to be. Many people assumed we would be going, indeed almost forced us to go, round the world for the second time. Certainly that was our aim, but we were shy of saying so in case some mishap or enforced change of plan defeated it. Although the more sensational Press is for ever sending small yachts off 'round the world', there are, so far as I know, still only five British yachts of under 40 tons ever to have made circumnavigations. However, in order to obtain permission from the Customs and Excise people to ship stores out of bond (we usually carry whisky, tobacco, and sometimes a case of rum), I had to give our proposed route for the first three months, and I mentioned Georgetown in British Guiana towards the end of that period. Permission was granted, provided we cleared for that port, which we did, and that had the merit of quietening the people who had no idea where it was and were too shy to ask. We had every intention of going there if we could find it, but it is not the easiest of landfalls because of the low coast, the off-lying shoals, and the strong current.

On Sunday, 19 July 1959, we slipped away from Yarmouth, but not unnoticed. Although we did not decide to go until we had eaten breakfast, the news spread rapidly. That week-end was fine and warm, and the little harbour was so packed with yachts that the lanes between the rows of piles were very narrow. As we made our way slowly through, several foghorns were sounded and some people came on deck to wish us good luck. Our friend Harold Hayles, coxswain of the life-boat and the only person to whom we had confided our real intention, escorted us a little way in his launch; one last wave, and the ebb hurried us out through Hurst Narrows. Our home port, of which we are very fond, slipped out of sight, and we were alone; we realized then how much of friendship and kindness we were leaving astern.

We slit open then the envelope given to us by the Royal Solent Yacht Club. It was marked 'To be opened after leaving Yarmouth', and the note it contained read:

The Flag Officers and Members of this Club wish Godspeed and *bon voyage* to their most distinguished honorary life members, Eric and Susan Hiscock, on their forthcoming cruise in *Wanderer III*.

2

South to the Cape Verdes

We had fine weather and light winds mostly from a westerly quarter all the way down Channel, so we did have to beat after all, but the coasts of Dorset, Devon, and Cornwall looked serene and lovely in the sunlight. We put into Falmouth briefly to have a defective skin fitting attended to, and then passed outside Ushant with a fair wind.

For the most part the Bay of Biscay treated us gently, and the 453-mile passage to La Coruña on the north-west corner of Spain took five and a half days.* However, we did have one twelve-hour period close-hauled under reduced sail, pitching heavily into a steep head-sea. Our shore-bound stomachs rebelled at such treatment, but with the help of Avomine managed to retain their churned-up contents, and we soon got into the old, well-remembered seagoing routine, in which our only unsolved problem is how to get enough sleep. Because of the difficulty of remaining awake when steering, we usually take watches of only two or two and a half hours, and although such short spells are kind to the helmsman, they do not allow the watch below a sufficiently long period of unbroken sleep, especially as there is often a call for all hands to make or take in sail. Our attempts to make this up by each having two hours in our bunks during the afternoon are not entirely successful, particularly in the tropics, when that is the hottest time of day, and tired though we may be, neither Susan nor I are good at sleeping in the daytime in spite of years of practice.

* All distances given in this book are in nautical miles of approximately 2,000 yards.

During that crossing of the Bay, however, we did have one night so calm when well clear of the shipping lane that we hung up the riding light and both turned in. That day, and by day I mean the period from ship's noon to ship's noon, which traditionally the seaman uses when computing the day's run, we made good only 23 miles; but that did not worry us, for after our sound sleep we were both full of renewed vigour and keen anticipation. As Susan, swaying to the motion, busied herself with her pots and pans, she sang happily, and when she does that I know that all is well with her and her galley.

With the exception of breakfast—which I always get because some years ago I was foolish enough to express my theory that cooking is not so difficult as housewives often pretend, and that it should be possible to cook and shave at the same time—Susan makes herself responsible for the preparation and cooking of all meals. Lunch on board is always cold, but the weather has to be bad indeed to prevent her from cooking the evening meal, although sometimes after she has done so she has not been able to eat much of it.

In fine weather I always enjoyed the pre-supper hour. Chocked off against the motion in the small self-draining cockpit, with one hand on the tiller and the other cradling my evening drink, I felt at peace. Except in coastal or ship-frequented waters we showed no navigation lights when one or other of us was on watch, and in the dark our ship looked larger and more important than she did in full daylight as she bustled along, the tall, dark silhouette of her sails swinging across the sky, the faintly luminous lace of the bow-wave slipping past with a hiss on either side to join again in the gurgling tumult of the wake. Close before me, sunk beneath a pane of unbreakable glass in the bridge deck, which separates cockpit from companionway, lay the three faint luminous lines of the compass grid, which had been set at noon, and all I had to do was steer so that the swinging north-south line stayed parallel between the other two.

The companionway hatch was open, and as Susan had lit the two gimballed cabin lamps, in the soft yellow light which picked out the highlights on varnish and enamel, I could see all of the inside of our small floating home. Four steps led down to its scrubbed, iroko-planked floor. Immediately to port was the galley with its stainless-steel-topped working bench, self-stowing racks for crockery, and lockers and drawers for other equipment and ready-use stores. At the forward end, swinging in its gimballs, was the two-burner Para-Fin stove, to which Susan was just putting a light—the appetizing smell of the pre-heating methylated spirit was in the air. Opposite was the hanging locker for oilskins, and the chart table with drawers beneath it, in which I knew 300 charts lay waiting ready to show us the way in to all manner of strange places. Beyond this, the working part of the ship, was the cabin proper, a space about 8 ft. square. On either side of the mahogany table was a settee berth with upholstered ends and back, all covered in green waterproof material with white piping. Over the forward end of each berth was a sideboard, on which were secured the sextant and chronometer boxes and the barograph; on one a pile of unread magazines was held by the fiddles. Our bedding was stowed in the space under each sideboard, and our feet went there when sleeping. The lower end of the 50 ft. hollow silver-spruce mast, which was painted white from truck to heel to help keep it cool in the tropics and so preserve the glue with which it was held together, came down between the side-boards; to reach the forepeak, where anchor chains, warps, lamps, and all the sails not in use were stowed, one had to squeeze round it, a feat which a few of our larger friends are unable to perform. Above the backrests, and running the full length of both berths, were tight-packed bookshelves, and on the bulkhead at the forward end, a few of our more highly prized possessions—a black-lip pearl shell from Tahiti, a Thurburn painting of the Helford River in the snow, the Blue Water Medal of the Cruising Club of America with both our names engraved on it. It all looked wonderfully bright and cosy, and in remarkable contrast to the night outside.

Susan came part way out of the hatch to empty the potato

peelings over the side. She paused for a moment, looking round, feeling the direction of the wind on her face.

'How're you doing out here?' she asked, her voice clear and rather exciting, just as I had always known it.

'Doing well, a good five knots. What's for supper?'

'Chips and onions. But what'll it be, steak and kidney or the old bangers?'

I did not much mind, so long as we were having chips, a favourite at sea with both of us, probably because it is often too rough for frying, and then we have to eat our potatoes boiled. 'It's a quiet night, so why not make it bangers; we can always have steak and kid. when it's rough.'

She slipped below; the frying-pan, an old friend we have had with us in all our boats, gleamed dully as she took it from the locker under the stove, and soon the appetizing aroma of frying drifted out of the hatch, the clean blue flame of the stove hissing beneath the pan.

I stood up, wedged my glass between the two parts of the wire runner, and looked all round. There was nothing to be seen except the dark, unsteady line of the horizon, and the stars. 'We're well outside the shipping lane,' I thought, as I settled myself again.

Presently Susan pulled on an anorac, came into the cockpit beside me and put her hand over mine on the tiller. 'I'd like a breath of fresh air before I eat,' she said, 'so you have yours first.'

I knew it was useless to argue, for this little act was always put on when there were chips for supper, because chips spoil with keeping. As I started to gobble mine down so that hers should not become too soft, Susan cried out:

'Slowly, slowly, sailor, there's plenty of time; we'll have three hundred nights at sea before we get back home.'

After an uneventful crossing of the Bay we entered La Coruña harbour in the dark, the entry being made the more anxious by reason of a fleet of open boats without lights fishing in the approaches, drizzle which at times obscured everything, and a new breakwater, not shown on the chart or properly described in the latest edition of the *Pilot*, sticking out from the western shore; there was no light at its seaward end. It is man-made alterations such as this, the changing of navigation lights, or the placing of unlighted obstructions, which make the night entry to a commercial or naval port so dangerous for the visitor without local knowledge. From a previous visit ten years before, we knew where the Club Nautico lay, and having got safely into the harbour, we went in search of it; but instead of the solid mass of the club house all we could see silhouetted against the night glow of the city in the sky was a network of masts and radar scanners. Eventually we discovered the basin beside the club; we motored cautiously in, found it very crowded, and enveloped in the powerful midnight smells and noises of a Spanish town, and let the anchor go.

In the morning, when we went on deck to make colours, we saw the bows of three men-of-war projecting beyond the club house—theirs were the masts and scanners we had seen in the night. Naturally we presumed them to be Spanish, but on the stroke of eight we watched with great pleasure as three Union flags ran up their jackstaffs. The ships proved to be the destroyers *Saintes*, *Armada*, and *Camperdown*, there to help commemorate the 150th anniversary of the burial of Sir John Moore, whose tomb, well shaded by trees, is in Carlos Gardens. The basin was so crowded and dirty, and its landing places so thickly coated with oil (today most commercial ports, both at home and abroad, present something of a landing problem in the form of filth, small boys, or the wash of passing craft) that we soon moved to a cleaner anchorage outside, where we lay under the eye of the Navy, and having made friends with *Camperdown*, the outermost of the three destroyers, landed at her white-scrubbed accommodation ladder and left our dinghy safely there.

A remarkable feature of the old, eastern, part of the town is the large number of buildings with projecting, small-paned, glass fronts, and these are in strong contrast to the dark buildings flanking the narrow back streets, where every fourth door-way, or so it seems, leads to a cool, dim bar with rows of huge wine barrels; and its vast bedlam of a market, with fish on the top floor, bread on the middle floor, and fruit and vegetables in colourful profusion on the ground floor, is a ship-wife's paradise. We spent some time there, and then relaxed in one of the stainless steel bathrooms and the fan-cooled wardroom of friendly *Camperdown.*

It was at La Coruña one afternoon, when the rays from the sun bounced back from the white pavements of the new town with heat and light enough to make one's eyeballs hurt and the sweat run down one's back, that we made our way with a swelling crowd to the Plaza de Toros to watch the bullfight. As the building is circular, and the fight may take place in any part of the arena, it matters little where one sits except that seats can be had either *sol* or *sombra.* As it was so hot, we paid extra for *sombra,* and were glad of it. The foreigner's reactions to this, the national sport of Spain, tend to be mixed, and naturally he cannot understand the finer points; my own feelings, having once worked with bulls and gained respect and admiration for them, were that the bull stands no chance at all; he appears bewildered, and for the most part makes no attempt to attack the matador, but only the purple cloak with which he is tormented. Clearly great skill and bravery are displayed by the matador, particularly when he interposes his brilliantly and immaculately clad person between the cloak and the lowered horns, but even if he is gored, and bullfighters often are, some-one else will kill the bull that afternoon. The introduction of a blindfold horse, just the right height for the bull to get his horns under, appears uncivilized, but, as I have said, there must be much more to all this than meets the casual eye. For us the saddest incident of the afternoon was when a none-too-bold matador, who with advancing years had lost something of his skill and nerve, was booed and clapped ironically by the impatient crowd. There were tears in his eyes as he hurried to the exit. We watched three of the four bulls slaughtered, their gory carcasses dragged from the arena in clouds of dust, while the crowd—of which a large proportion was female—cheered loudly and tossed hats, handbags, and skins of wine at the feet of the victorious matadors. Feeling a little sick, we then left and came away through the dim, urine-impregnated tunnels, and had some difficulty in letting ourselves out of the locked building.

From La Coruña we made our way west and south round Finisterre and down the coast of Spain, stopping at several places which we had visited on earlier cruises and, height of luxury for us, spending each night at anchor. So we came eventually to the mouth of Arosa Bay, the most interesting of the four great inlets which penetrate that part of Spain. As we headed in for it in misty weather, when we could see none of the mountain peaks which should serve to give the seaman his position, we fell in with a fleet of twenty-four small fishing boats, each bulging with men, casting their nets in one small area of the sea—it looked as though the entire male population of a village had put to sea and was still continuing the village gossip. We made our way 10 miles up the bay to an anchorage off Puebla del Caramiñal, the buildings of which topped a crescent beach of sand and shells, splashed with vivid colour in the low evening light.

The place, which makes its living entirely on sea-food—tunny, sardines, and mussels, all of which are canned there—proved to be so attractive and friendly, and so typical of the smaller Spanish coastal towns, that we decided to make a movie sequence of Susan shopping in the little market by the fountain, where smiling, weather-beaten women in black preside over the stalls or fetch water from the fountain in metal-bound containers balanced on their heads. That little bit of photography cost us nearly a week in planning, rehearsing, and waiting for the right weather and lighting. We were beginning to realize that indiscriminate shooting was just a waste of expensive film; that the telling of a story on the screen, with the need for close-ups, long shots, cuts, and change of camera angle, was a different language, and one that we had got to learn if our finished film was to be of interest to anyone but ourselves. However, we consoled ourselves by remembering that it took five professionals, with a lot of costly equipment and a motor launch in constant attendance, eight hours to make a

five-minute film for television of *Wanderer* and ourselves before
we left Yarmouth. That was an interesting and instructive
experience for us, and at times an amusing one. With all five
men clustered on the foredeck, the huge camera on a steel
tripod straddling the coachroof, and a tape-recorder together
with a batch of accumulators hidden below, *Wanderer* went for
an afternoon sail in the Solent. The flood was making and the
wind was ahead, so we had to tack many times, and each time
we put about all the gear had to be rearranged. That film unit
even brought its own actor along.

Arosa Bay is one of those jolly, but now rare, places where
there are usually many little sailing and rowing boats about;
some spend their time fishing, others ferry the women and
children from one village to another, or bring loads of timber
for the making of fish boxes, while a few attend to the peculiar
industry of rearing mussels. This consists of binding young
mussels with a netting of string to 18-ft. lengths of stout rope, a
few feet at the end of each rope being left bare. The ropes are
then suspended vertically from rafts moored in the bay, and are
left there for a year. In that time the small mussels grow to full
size ready for canning, and a colony of young forms on the naked
part of the rope to provide the nucleus of the next year's crop.

We called at several other places on the Spanish coast, most
of which we had visited before, and then sailed down the
Portuguese coast to Leixoes (pronounced something like
'Leshoinge'), the port for the city of Oporto. It is an artificial
harbour, formed by two massive breakwaters with a third, in-
complete and awash at low tide, projecting in a south-westerly
direction, its outer end marked by a small lighthouse. As we
approached this and hardened our sheets for the beat in against
the strong north wind, several motor fishing vessels came out
and rounded it. If we had had any idea of what was to follow
we would have stood out to sea for the next half-hour or so;
but unaware we headed on in. The Leixoes sardine fleet consisted at that time of 148 fine, rakish-looking vessels, each with
a crew of thirty men, or more; the entire fleet puts to sea at
about 6 p.m. each week-day and returns in the early hours of

the morning. We arrived at 6 p.m. precisely, and out round the blind corner of the high eastern breakwater at a good 12 knots came the fleet in bunches of a dozen or so, each crew shouting as it worked together to haul the punt up on to the low round stern. With all the wind she wanted under full sail, *Wanderer* went storming in among them, pitching in their confused wash and deluging herself with spray. To add to the general confusion as we approached, a dredger, which had been at work in the lee of the sunken breakwater, chose that moment to get her anchors and proceed to sea to dump her load of sand. The scene was exciting, full of brilliant colour and vigorous activity, but we were glad to get into the harbour without mishap, and under power make our way to the inner basin, where there was much coming and going of punts with gunwales almost awash, ferrying crews to the late starters.

With the help of a boatman who spoke a little English, we shopped in the town, where the boisterous wind raised miniature sandstorms, sharp and stinging, and we took the No. 1 tram, which runs beside the River Douro, into Oporto, a stately, unhurried journey except when we had to mount a hill which can only be taken at a run; three times our tram was balked by other vehicles and had to descend to the bottom and try again, but as few of the passengers so much as lifted their eyes from their newspapers, we presumed this to be a common occurrence. We walked out on the upper span of the high bridge across the Douro from which a lower bridge is suspended, and watched the barges, each with a single jet-black squaresail, moving like toys on the brown water of the river far below, a river which in certain conditions can rise as much as 14 ft. above normal high-water level, and attain a speed of 16 knots.

We called at other places in Portugal, the most enjoyable of them being Barreiro at the head of a creek on the southern shore of the River Tagus. The Reynolds, who are friends of ours, own a cork factory there, and when they heard we were coming Tony Reynolds and his boatman met us and piloted us in, for the creek is narrow and tortuous, and does not often have to accommodate a vessel drawing as much as *Wanderer* does. At its head we secured alongside the outer wall of the boathouse where Tony's 10-tonner lay in the shade with her mast protruding through a slit in the roof. For several days we lay there, taking the ground for nine hours out of every twelve, and each evening we dined at the candle-lit table in the Reynolds' hospitable home, deriving much pleasure from speaking and listening to our own language for a change. The Portuguese trade wind—the name is given to the north wind because of the constancy with which it blows along this coast—died away on the evening of our arrival, so we found it very hot on board, and dusty because of our nearness to the cork mill which hummed day and night, its note rising and falling in cadence like that of a threshing drum. But a few yards away within the Reynolds' *quinta* lay a pale green, shady swimming pool of fresh water, where we went to cool off several times a day in company with the other inhabitants of that small British oasis. From our awning-shaded deck we could look out beyond the sand spit and the creek to where the grey sails and brilliantly coloured hulls of the *frigatas*, the engineless barges of the Tagus, drifted on the tide.

For more than a week the wind was dead, but as soon as it showed signs of renewed life we said good-bye to our kind friends, slipped out of the Tagus, and after spending a night at Sesimbra took our departure for Casablanca in Morocco.

We were now sailing in waters new to us, and as the light on Cape St. Vincent dipped below the horizon astern we felt that our adventure was really beginning; much, no doubt, would happen before we raised that powerful flashing light again—if all went well we would first have drawn a line round the world—when we would raise it coming from the east as we left the Strait of Gibraltar astern.

For the greater part of the 305-mile trip to Casablanca the wind, which was abaft the beam all the way, was so light that it could not keep the mainsail asleep; but we noticed that the terylene sail did not slam so violently as the old heavier cotton one had done in similar conditions. Otherwise the weather was good with cloudless days and star-filled nights.

The *Africa Pilot*, Vol. I, gives a list of conspicuous objects useful to the mariner approaching Casablanca—a water tower, a chimney, and some radio masts. But the first things we saw through the afternoon haze were the white mass of the town itself and some ships at anchor inside the mile-long breakwater, which soon lifted above the sea. As we neared the whistle buoy off the breakwater's end, a small sailing boat came bounding out to meet us.

'Welcome to Morocco,' cried her helmsman. 'Go straight on to the basin at the far end.'

That is what we did, and there were helped to secure between buoys off the friendly Société Nautique by Group Captain ('Call me Leigh') Rankin from the neighbouring yacht, the schooner *Penella*, flying the Australian ensign. He and his wife Dorrie had set out from England the previous autumn to sail round the world and visit their children and grandchildren in various places, but they left their departure until rather late, encountered some very bad weather which exhausted them and carried their steering gear away, and they were towed by a salvage tug into Casablanca. Undaunted they had completed repairs during the winter and now were just about to continue their voyage.

The greater part of the town, with its wide streets, modern buildings, and shops laid out largely to attract the tourist, had little appeal for us; but the Medina, the original French town and now the Arab quarter, with its narrow, crooked alleys, its pungent smells, and its teeming population, we found foreign and fascinating. One evening Jean Pierre Cuny and his wife Marie-José (her long blonde hair would have been the pride of any Scandinavian girl) invited us out to dinner, and at our request took us to an eating house in the Medina. The place was astonishingly ill cared for; neither the room, which was filled with a blue haze of smoke, nor the table at which we ate appeared to have been cleaned for many a day, and immedi-

---

PLATE 3
The market square of the fishing town of Caramiñal, where the fountain provides the only freshwater supply.

ately fresh paper napkins were spread on the table they became discoloured with the soup and wine of previous meals. However, the food was interesting and good, particularly the barbecued meat, which was cooked on open fires in the same room and eaten from the fingers off skewers, and the smoke from the fires kept the flies away. It was an uproariously jolly evening in most entertaining company, and when I asked Jean Pierre, who was a local journalist, if the Medina was still considered a dangerous place for the stranger by night, he replied: '*A deux heures—tonk!*' and he went through the motions of striking me on the head and rifling my pockets.

Our intention being to work our way along the little-visited coast of Morocco until we neared the Canary Islands, we did not stay long at Casablanca, for civil disturbances appeared to be brewing, and the British Consul, when we visited him to collect our mail, advised us to leave the country by 20 September. We beat out of the harbour, escorted by friends, after a stay of six days, and sailed away to the west and south. After two days and a night of coasting we entered the artificial harbour of Safi, which we judged from the chart to be one of the best in Morocco, but were badly mistaken. We entered it in the dark and made our way cautiously under power to the inner part, which is narrow, and was made even narrower that night by a tightly packed fleet of fishing vessels, lying at each side, bows to the walls, anchors out astern. We let go in an uncomfortably restricted berth between them, and when we had switched off the engine there was an uncanny silence, broken only by the sinister sucking of the swell, and an occasional long-drawn-out shriek, as of an animal in pain, when the wooden sides of the fishing vessels ground against one another. Silently, almost stealthily it seemed, boats passed to and fro. Nobody spoke, and the sense of foreboding was heightened by the consumptive cough of a fisherman—he was still coughing at

PLATE 4
Top: A sunlit street in Mogador. Long-robed men, veiled women . . . untouched by modern civilization. *Bottom:* Agadir. The old town on the hill-top, and the new—both were destroyed by the earthquake with a loss of 10,000 lives.
B.W.H.–C

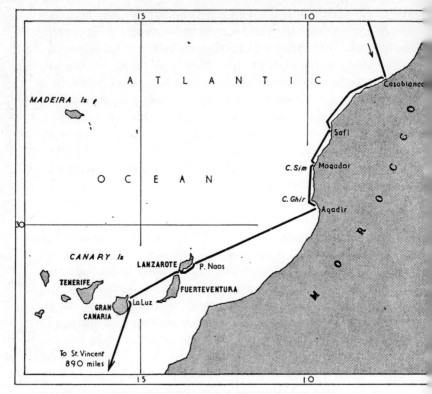

MOROCCO AND CANARY ISLANDS

daybreak. The stench of decaying fish and sewage was nauseating. We spent an uneasy night with our only weapon, a twelve-bore shotgun, loaded in readiness to repel boarders, then I put Susan ashore to buy a loaf of bread and a can of petrol, and succeeded in getting both of us and the dinghy foul with the thick black oil with which the walls and landing places glistened slimily. As soon as she returned we left, having no wish to prolong our stay in such a depressing place, and it was a great relief to get out into the clean ocean with a fresh breeze blowing from the north, after the stink and filth of the port, and as we hurried south we killed the evil, black, fat flies which had boarded us at Safi; but for the time being we could do nothing about the smell which had come aboard with the anchor chain and now pervaded the forepeak.

We were bound for Mogador, 60 miles along the coast. This is the only attempt made by nature to provide a natural harbour on the coast of Morocco; there an indentation in the low, sandy coastline is partly protected by an island and reefs, but by all accounts a heavy sea rolls in with strong onshore winds. The ruins of several Portuguese forts on shore, rocks, and island show that the place was once of some importance; indeed, Francis Drake put in there during his circumnavigation. The chart showed that a small walled harbour had been built on the northern shore, but this appeared to be too shallow for us.

Along this coast a low glass is often accompanied by a heavy swell from north-west, associated with depressions moving across the North Atlantic. So it was that day, and when in the evening the wind fell light and we could hear all too clearly the thunder of surf on the shore, and later see it, a ribbon of white, in the light of the full moon, we seriously wondered whether conditions were suitable for paying a visit to Mogador.

We arrived off the harbour in the dark, and deciding not to attempt to enter until daylight, we hove-to for several hours. In that short time, and with a rising glass, the swell moderated remarkably, and at dawn we sailed into the roadstead and anchored on a sandy bottom, south-east of the entrance to the fishing-boat harbour. The wind was north-east, and we rolled heavily to the swell to which we were lying beam on, for it was only partly broken by a reef which covered at high water. We found ourselves in unusual and beautiful surroundings. To the north of us lay the walled town, a fine jumble of white and cream flat-roofed houses, minarets, and forts. East and south of us curved a broad beach of golden sand backed by white sandhills over which some camels were making their swaying way. The coast faded out of sight in the haze towards Cape Sim 9 miles to the south. On the chart the neighbourhood of that coast is devoid of soundings; the symbol for breakers is shown together with the one word 'unsurveyed'. To the south-west lay the island on which stood a fort, a tomb—tombs, most of which looked much alike to us, are practically the only landmarks along this featureless desert shore—and a minaret. To the west lay the open sea, and to the north-west the reef on which the swell was piling. The scents were those of sand and spice, of sardines and camel dung. Had the weather been calm we would probably have seen the snow-capped Atlas mountains from where we lay; but that is never possible when the wind is fresh, for there is always some haze then. After breakfast we launched the dinghy with difficulty because of the rolling, and taking the cameras along, rowed into the harbour and landed. As soon as our backs were turned the dinghy was pounced upon by a party of children; but a lean old man drove them away and indicated that he would act as watchman while we were ashore. A policeman (or he may have been a soldier) escorted us at a very slow pace, which was perhaps more in keeping with the fierce heat then beating down than is our own impatient shore-going stride, to a huge, cool, dim building, which may have been the police station. There our passports were studied minutely and discussed by several officials, and as we could speak no word of the language, we could not explain the reason for our visit. Obviously visitors were rare at Mogador. We were impatient to see the town and get back on board, but in Morocco, as in other Arab countries, time means very little, and we had to be patient. But within the hour, and after many smiles and gestures of friendliness, we were free to do as we wished, and explored the town, where the sun poured heat and light and cast deep shadows. Off the wider, sunlit streets branched narrow darker ones on either side of which were black archways leading to windowless dwellings, and there were people, people everywhere, long-robed men, veiled women, and many children. There was something timeless about the place; we felt that it was practically untouched by modern civilization—we did not see one single motor vehicle, we heard no radio, and the shops displayed goods that were strange to us. The older people had a noticeable grace and courtesy.

Next day when we sailed out of the roadstead our intention was to spend a night in the anchorage the chart showed in the lee of Cape Sim, but by the time we reached the cape the sky looked so dirty, with much greasy cloud working up from the south-west, that we decided to keep away from the land. It was as well that we did so, for at 6.30 p.m. things began to happen fast. The rapidly freshening wind called for double reefs immediately, i.e. a reduction of more than half the area of the mainsail, but half an hour later there was too much wind even for that, so we handed it and set the trysail (only 75 sq. ft.), and fearing from the run of the clouds that the wind might back and make the coast a dangerous lee shore, we altered course more to seaward. With the wind on her quarter *Wanderer* ran fast, and was fairly steady in her motion and easy on the helm, for the sea had not yet had a chance to get up. But an hour later the sea had grown steep and crested and the wind was still increasing, so we took in the trysail and ran on almost as fast, at about 6 knots, under the small staysail alone. Yet we soon had to take in even that, and rounding up we lay a-hull, i.e. beam on to wind and sea, with the sudden violent gale roaring in the rigging with an impressive note of power and fury. At that time we were in company with a small fleet of what we took to be sardiners. They, like ourselves, were lying a-hull, but with less draught and greater windage were drifting to leeward faster, and it was necessary to keep a check on them.

This was the first really bad weather we had experienced since leaving England, and I think the wind reached whole gale force between 9 and 11 p.m., when the barograph drew a sharp V on its chart; but fortunately it did not last for long, and soon after midnight there was only a light breeze. However, the sea was so confused and the motion so violent that I shirked the job of making full sail until daylight, when we rounded Cape Ghir and found quieter water. But it did us little good, for the wind became fickle and then died, and fog, grey and clammy, rolled in from seaward. So we motored the remaining 15 miles to Agadir, but with some misgiving because we had no wish to overrun our objective and find ourselves among the breakers on the desert coast south of that port. Shortly before noon, through one of those strange tunnels of clear air which are sometimes met with in a fog, Susan saw the old walled town of Agadir high above the harbour, and got a bearing of it before it vanished again. Our troubles were then over, and soon afterwards we came to an anchorage in the harbour which the French had recently completed, thankful to be in, for almost at once the fog shut down again thicker than ever, and remained so until dusk.

The old town was perched on the summit of the 770-ft. hill which dominated the harbour, and with its castellated walls and minarets it looked like a fairy castle. One hot afternoon we made our way on foot up the zigzag road and so came to the town's single entrance, in the dark archways of which loitered a crowd of dirty, ill-nourished children; most of them had skin complaints, their scalps and limbs disfigured by scabs and running sores. An Arab in some sort of uniform attached himself to us and insisted on showing us round the usual things, the look-out tower, the ramparts, and the shop which offered leather goods and rugs at high prices; but we were determined to see the dwellings, and were shocked at what we saw—the overcrowding and the poverty; the lack of light and sanitation; the flies crawling, apparently unnoticed, on the faces of the people; and the smells. Yet here, as at Mogador, there was a certain grace and dignity, a suggestion that the present was of no importance. We wondered, as we made our way down the steep short cut among the cacti, just what the inhabitants of old Agadir thought of the new Agadir sprawled on the plain below them, at whose modern shops, shiny cars, and tourist hotels they could gaze all day, for they appeared to have little else to do.

It was good to return to *Wanderer*'s clean, sweet-smelling cabin and have a wash, but old Agadir reminded us of her presence throughout our stay. Not only could we see her from our anchorage, a whited sepulchre bright in the sunlight high above us, but every morning before dawn the voice of the holy man, bidding the people to prayer from a minaret, came floating clearly down to wake us—high pitched, long drawn out, sharply ended. It made our scalps prick.

A few months after our visit an earthquake, followed as such things so often are by a tidal wave, did untold damage to Agadir, and more than 10,000 people were killed, many of them being buried alive. The Crown Prince of Morocco, Moulay Hassan, ordered what little remained of the town to be destroyed because of the risk of plague and other diseases from the hordes of rats.

Departing from Agadir, we left the African coast obliquely, and sailing in a west-south-west direction made the 225-mile passage to Lanzarote, the easternmost of the Canary Islands. The trip was a real pleasure. The weather was fine, there was a moderate fair wind, and so little sea that it seemed we could be only just within the northern verge of the north-east trade-wind belt. We were bound for Lanzarote because the chart showed it to possess the only natural harbour in the archipelago, a small indentation on the south-east coast called Port Naos, which appeared to be protected from seaward, and the *Pilot* confirmed this, by reefs and a small island. We arrived by night and jilled about until dawn, then went in by the western entrance, but were dismayed to find the place so filled with large, and apparently derelict, trading ketches and schooners that it was with some difficulty that we managed to work our way in to a restricted berth among them. There we lay rolling as heavily as they on the swell which came in through both entrances, met in the middle and boomed along the rocky shores.

There was something impressively abandoned about the roll of those large sailing vessels; at one moment their splintered and paintless bulwarks were within a few feet of the water, and the next we could see a huge expanse of weed- and barnacle-encrusted bilge. It seemed that little *Wanderer* might almost be overlaid by her ungainly neighbours, each of which had three anchors down, suggesting to us that the holding ground was poor. Two shore boats came off to hang on to us limpet fashion, their occupants indicating that we would be safer in Arrecife Harbour just round the corner. We thought so, too, but we had got ourselves into such a tight berth that extrication with certainty would only be possible under power, and it took me the best part of two hours to make the motor go, so reluctant was it to start on the petrol we had bought at Agadir, which I suspected of being diluted with paraffin.

We found that Arrecife was just as crowded and almost as rough as Port Naos, so we sailed on our way along the south side of the island, enjoying the jaunty, colourful volcanic peaks, which reminded us of Ascension Island, intending to pass through the strait between Lanzarote and Fuerteventura and so reach La Luz, which is the port for Las Palmas on Grand Canary. But in the strait we were so attracted by a bay on the northern side that we beat into it, following the line of soundings taken by H.M.S. *Etna* in 1835, and there spent an undisturbed night at anchor on a sandy bottom, out of sight of human habitation except for the winking lighthouses at each end of the strait. That was the first silent and completely relaxing night we had enjoyed for several weeks. We sailed away in the morning with regret, and made a swift passage across to Grand Canary, raising the great light on La Isleta before midnight. By then we had jettisoned our suspect petrol, and not feeling prepared to beat into the artificial harbour of La Luz in the dark, we hove-to until daylight—that, it seemed, was becoming a habit of ours—and then sailed in with the greatest of ease to anchor in the inner basin among the other Atlantic candidates, an American, a German, a Frenchman, and two English single-handers.

We stayed for six days in that dirty and not very interesting place because there was no wind, and were there for the total eclipse of the sun on 1 October. The day was cloudy and many people had gone across to Fuerteventura, for that island is less than half the height of Grand Canary, and it was thought that there would be a better chance of a clear sky there. In mid-morning the light began to wane, and then miraculously a big patch of clear sky appeared and we were able to watch the moon encroaching on the sun's face, and we took turns looking at it through the shades of the sextant. As the morning grew darker a hush spread over La Luz. I cannot believe that the roaring traffic really did stop, though it sounded as though that had happened, but certainly the dogs which every coaster and fishing boat had aboard, and which normally barked from dawn to dusk, were silent, and we could hear the twilight talk of birds. When the sun had been completely covered by the moon it looked just like a photograph we have at home taken by Susan's father, who was a Fellow of the Royal Astronomical Society, many years ago—a black disk with light streamers of varying shape and intensity (the solar prominences) radiating from behind it, a lovely and impressive sight. The eclipse was total for about two minutes, then the moon moved slowly on and gradually daylight returned. As the light increased, so La Luz came to life, and very soon, just as though there had never been that remarkable display by nature, the traffic rolled and roared, the people shouted, and the dogs resumed their harsh, hot, angry barking.

From La Luz to St. Vincent in the Cape Verde Islands is about 900 miles, and we covered that distance in $8\frac{1}{4}$ days, in spite of being held motionless for 24 hours in the calm which high Grand Canary creates in her lee. There was very little swell, so the calm was not unpleasant, and before we became bored with it an air stole upon us from the north-east, strengthening slowly, and soon we had *Wanderer* steering herself under her twin spinnakers. On the fourth day she made a run of 140 miles, the best that she has ever made under those small sails, the combined area of which is only 250 sq. ft. But the wind continued to freshen, and the next day we took in one of the twins, and under the other, having to steer then, made a day's run of 120 miles; we were making southing fast, too fast for peace of mind and comfort. The weather generally seemed out of sorts; there was a steeper and heavier sea than is usually found in trade-wind areas, the ship rolled so violently that she repeatedly dipped each rail in turn deep into the sea; the sky had a gloomy appearance, and though it was not overcast, or much clouded, it was veiled; sun and moon had haloes, and the stars no brilliance.

I, as navigator, supposed that St. Vincent would be easy enough to find, for it is not low, and its near neighbour, Santo

Antão, stands 4,000 ft. high. But as we approached I began to
wonder about the accuracy of my sights, for the sky continued
to be hazed, and the horizon was indistinct and had a yellowish
band extending about 10 deg. above it, just as though the air
was filled with desert sand as it is during an harmattan. But
October is not normally a harmattan month.

During the afternoon of our eighth day at sea, and after
taking sights which put us close, but might be suspect, up in
the sky fine on the starboard bow appeared the indistinct grey
outline of Santo Antão's peaks, and soon after the conical hills
of St. Vincent appeared ahead.

Once again we made a night arrival and were bewildered by
lights and unlighted obstructions which were not shown on the
chart or mentioned in the latest supplement to the *Pilot*. Next
day we discovered these to be in connexion with a new breakwater then building, the submerged part of which constituted a
grave danger to the stranger by night. However, we managed
to puzzle our anxious way in to an anchorage in the large bay
of Porto Grande, where almost at once we were visited by a pilot.

'Keep a good watch, captain,' he said; 'plenty thieves.'

At dawn he came to us again and kindly showed us to a more
sheltered berth among the picturesque inter-island trading
schooners and cutters, some of which were so decrepit that we
wondered how they ever managed to make the open sea passages
between the islands, each with a high deck cargo and passengers
perched atop of that.

Since coal for bunkering was abandoned in favour of fuel
oil St. Vincent has fallen on lean days, with almost no employ-
ment for the rapidly increasing population. Theft is therefore
common, and the thieves are quite brazen about it. It is said
that a ship in for bunkers had one of her life-boats stolen, and
that next day that same life-boat, painted a different colour,
was seen afloat in the bay. Yachts are also considered to be
fair game. The ketch *Scolopax* employed a watchman when her
people were ashore, but he stole the food out of the cans in her
lockers and inverted the empties so that the theft was not discovered until the yacht was on her way to Galveston, Texas, and

being then in the heel of the north-east trade could scarcely
return.

We also employed a watchman each time we accepted the
kindly hospitality of the small British community ashore, but,
with *Scolopax* in mind, we locked the ship and left him on deck.
He always arrived early, perhaps in hope of earning a few extra
escudos, and sat in the cockpit intently watching every movement Susan and I made as we washed ourselves and changed
into our shore-going clothes.

The poverty of these people is pathetic. Because there was
no safe place at which to leave our dinghy, we usually employed
a shore boat to take us to the landing place, and when we
returned aboard the same boat took our watchman ashore.
One night after we had dined pleasantly with the British Consul
and his wife and had returned to *Wanderer*, the shore boat
brought our watchman back.

'Please may I have my sandwich?' he said.

I found it on the bridge deck, just a hunk of very stale bread.

Once Susan threw our own old and mildewed bread over the
side, and we were distressed to see three boats at once put out
from neighbouring coasters to salvage it and wolf it down,
sodden though it was with salt water. But, saddest thing of all,
due to complete lack of rain that year, the maize crop, which
provides the bulk of the islanders' diet, had failed, and fields
which should have been green with young shoots were brown
and barren. There is no water supply on St. Vincent, and every
drop has to be brought from Santo Antão by barge.

The Portuguese surveying ship *Comandante Almeida Carvalho*
was at anchor in the bay, taking a short rest from her work
among the islands, and we experienced much kindness from
her captain and officers. One evening they gave a dinner party
aboard for us, and in the course of conversation Susan happened
to mention that we had not been able to buy any good white
wine at St. Vincent. The Captain said nothing, but the boat
that carried us back to *Wanderer* late that night carried also
three five-litre *garafons* of Sanguinhal, a present from the ship.

3

The Atlantic
and British Guiana

The Atlantic crossing from the Cape Verdes is the shortest of the southern routes, 2,100 miles to Barbados as against 2,700 from the Canaries and 3,000 from Madeira. However, we were bound not for Barbados but for the Demerara River in British Guiana, the only British colony in South America, distant about 2,000 miles. We left St. Vincent on 19 October, getting a cheer from each of the inter-island vessels as we sailed past, and with a fresh north-east wind made runs of 131 miles on each of the first two days, quickly getting away from the islands and the shipping lanes and out into the empty ocean.

Both Susan and I are very conscious of the serious results which might attend personal injury, such as a burn or a broken limb, when on a long passage away from medical aid, and normally we are careful to an almost laughable degree. But during our second night out I had a small accident which served to remind me of the importance of constant care. I was very sleepy as I sat to windward steering, so sleepy that I omitted to put a line round myself, and Susan was so sleepy that she forgot to ask me whether I had done so. Presently I dozed off and pitched across to the lee side of the cockpit, knocking myself out when my head came in contact with, I think, the sheet winch; at the same time a large area of skin was ripped off my forearm. After I had recovered from the shock with a lump the size of a chicken's egg on my head, I considered how easily it might have been an eye that got damaged, or how, unconscious, I might have slipped overboard beneath the guardrail—and Susan would never have known how it happened. After that neither of us forgot our personal lifelines for some considerable time.

During the third day the wind hauled a little more easterly and moderated; we took in the mainsail, set the twin spinnakers, and after adjusting the braces to her liking, got *Wanderer* to steer herself for the next eight days, during which she averaged 105 miles a day. It was fortunate that the wind remained so steady in direction, for the twins are very limited in their activity, and will only work properly when the wind is almost dead astern. As they have no steadying effect the ship rolls violently, but we prefer to put up with that rather than the burden of steering. Besides, there is something particularly satisfying about running under twins: the wind is free, there is no need to stand watches, and there is no chafe or wear on the gear or sails—one seems to be getting something for nothing. Apart from the motion, which is tiring and tiresome, we spent an enjoyable and interesting time. We dealt with a few small jobs that needed attention, and then did a lot of photography in an attempt to show what our daily life was like for the amusement of our friends, and we did some filming and tape-recording which we hoped might be suitable for television; but that, with a 25-deg. roll every two seconds, is a job for an acrobat. The filming took a great deal of time in both planning and execution, and during those eight days we did little else except navigate, eat, and sleep, and we even talked films when we woke up in the night and had a look round on deck to see that the riding light was burning brightly and all was well.

One of our main filming problems was that we had no cameraman, so except on the rare occasion when we could use a tripod and a delayed-action release, it was not possible for both of us to appear in the picture at the same time; yet it was necessary to give the impression that we did so appear. A simple piece of action such as Susan passing some bananas out through the hatch and myself taking and eating them, required much rehearsal and an exchange of camera and bananas at the crucial moment, together with a change of lens and stop. Shots taken in the cabin sometimes had to be exposed at 8 frames per second instead of 24, at which rate the rest was shot, because of the poor light there and the slow speed of the colour film we were using; all action then had to be slowed down proportionally, and that entailed a lot of rehearsal timed with a stopwatch. There were times when the difficulties seemed insuperable and we almost abandoned filming, but in the end we were glad that we persevered, for after we had returned home the B.B.C. televised some of our film in two half-hour programmes, and as at the time *Wanderer* happened to be on exhibition at the International Boat Show at Earl's Court, London, a great many people spoke to us about the film. This seemed to have given them much pleasure, and that our artful dodges had been a success was proved by the number of visitors who commented that we must surely have had a cameraman on board, insisting, when questioned, that they had seen us both on the screen at the same time. Another handicap was that we did not see more than a very few of the 8,000 ft. of film we exposed until the voyage was finished. Colour film can so easily be harmed by heat and humidity after exposure that at the earliest opportunity we sent the reels of film by air mail for processing, after which they went to Peter Guinness, a fellow member of the Royal Cruising Club and a film expert. He and his wife kindly viewed it on their own screen, reported on the mistakes we had made, offered suggestions for improvement in the future, and kept it safely for us.

As we progressed to the westward, the wind surprisingly hauled farther round until it was south of east, and instead of the north-east swell one would expect in the heart of the north-east trade wind, it came from a south-easterly direction, giving the impression that the doldrums had been overcome by the south-east trade wind which was now penetrating far over on the north side of the Equator. The sky, too, was unusual. There were none of the puffy little clouds one associates with trade-wind weather; more often the sky was hazed over or scratched with thin cirrus, much as it had been off the African coast, and squalls of rain, sometimes accompanied by gusts of near gale force, became more frequent as we made westing. The only ship we saw was a tanker quite close when we were both enveloped in one of those squalls; we saw no fish except flying fish chased by sleepy-seeming porpoises, and the only birds were the ubiquitous storm petrels.

Not until we were approaching the South American coast and were beginning to think seriously about our landfall did the wind go back into the north-east, where it belonged. But that, of course, made the coast of British Guiana a lee shore, and we wondered what would happen when the big seas of the open ocean began to feel the bottom, for the water is very shallow for many miles offshore. The *Pilot* gave us little information beyond the fact that the rollers there are dangerous to heavily laden small craft (we supposed that *Wanderer* came into that category), but added that there are no rollers where the bottom is soft.

The Demerara River is not the easiest thing to find without the aid of a direction-finding radio set (at that time we didn't have one), for the coast of British Guiana is flat, low, and lacking in conspicuous objects, and the approach buoy, the East G.T., which we had to find, is not very large and it lies 10 miles from and therefore out of sight of land. If we failed to sight that buoy and stood on a bit too far, we might find ourselves among the shallow banks off the mouth of the Essequibo River, the graveyard of many a ship, as is shown by the number of wrecks on the chart. An additional anxiety is caused by the South Equatorial Current sweeping to the west-north-west at a rate of between 1 and 4 knots, and the tidal streams which run between the southern limit of that current and the coast.

We therefore took every opportunity of fixing our position by sun and star observations, fearful always that the sky might cloud over, which it showed every sign of being about to do again and again. The forenoon of our nineteenth day at sea found us sailing in thick, muddy, light-brown water. During the night the swell had died miraculously without a sign of a roller or the slightest confusion—probably this was due to the fact that we had made our approach where the chart showed the bottom to be of soft mud—and now, although there was no visible land, we might, so far as the size of sea was concerned, have been sailing in a large area of enclosed water.

I was fortunate in getting good sights of the sun that morning, and at noon was able to say to Susan: 'The East G.T. should now lie 25 miles ahead; we ought to sight it about 4.30 if this wind holds.' And to my intense relief we did. I never cease to marvel at the fact that I can fix my position on the surface of this small globe by spying on something so distant as the sun, or so infinitely distant as the stars, and at such times as my predicted landfalls work out satisfactorily I feel humble and most grateful to the men who have made such a thing possible. The buoy is a small, openwork affair, and not, you may say, a very large target at the end of a 2,000-mile trip; but, of course, the only sights that really matter are the last set one has taken.

Our navigational worries were then over, for 8 miles ahead stood a light beacon and beyond it several lighted buoys leading to the river's mouth. Night was upon us before we made the entrance where, with a sluicing flood under us and the trade wind moderated to a gentle breeze, we slipped quickly in past the lights of Georgetown (the capital) and of ships at anchor, and dropped our hook out of everybody's way near the western bank off a row of fishing stakes, which stood out clearly in the beam from our searchlight. The night was still and silent, and after we had stowed the sails and hung up the riding light, we remained relaxed on deck for a little while, listening to the crickets and whistling frogs, and inhaling the sugar-heavy perfume of British Guiana.

There is no good anchorage for small craft off Georgetown because of the river traffic and strong tidal streams, but next morning we moved across the river, which was so thick with

PLATE 5
Running under the twin rig. The wind is free, there is no need to steer, and there is no chafe on the gear or sails—one seems to be getting something for nothing.

suspended sediment that the shadows of mast and rigging lay bold and clear-cut on its surface as though on solid ground, to a temporary anchorage off the Sailing Club. The President of the Club at once called, and he introduced us to Major Atkinson, the Fire Chief, who kindly organized a berth for *Wanderer* between piles at the fire wharf, where she lay surrounded by fire-floats to protect her from the barges of sugar and rafts of greenheart logs which came drifting down on the ebb, and with smart firemen to guard her and help her crew in every possible way. There started that day such a round of hospitality and entertainment as we have rarely experienced outside New Zealand, and it continued without a break throughout our fortnight's stay in British Guiana.

The country is about the same size as Britain, but with less than one-hundredth of the population, of which about 90 per cent live and work on the narrow, flat coastal strip which is mostly used for the growing of sugar cane; there the neat fields of the plantations are sharply ruled by drainage and transport canals—the manatee, the tropical American sea-cow, has been imported to keep them free of weed—and dominated by the smoking chimneys of the sugar factories. Strangely enough the chart shows more than a hundred of the plantations with their names—Better Hope, Paradise, La Bon Intention, Profit, Success, Covent Garden, Mary and Harlem, etc. Behind the littoral is the bush, teeming with insect and reptile life, home of the deadly bushmaster, and beyond the bush the forest, vast, dark, and silent. The rivers are the highways, but so luxuriant is the growth of vegetation that many of the creeks leading off the rivers are completely grown over, dark tunnels invisible from the air. The country is rich in minerals, of which bauxite (the basis of aluminium) is the most important. Through the kindness of the British community we were enabled to see something of all these things.

The members of Georgetown Sailing Club, unlike those of

PLATE 6
Steering herself towards the sunset, the ship heads always for a point beyond the west horizon.

B.W.H.–D

most other such clubs with whom we have come in contact, did not try to persuade us. to go sailing with them. Instead they chartered a plane, an old cargo-carrying D.C.3, and twenty-three of them took the two of us for a flight inland over the green and trackless forest to have a picnic lunch on the borders of Brazil—they even provided a huge tub filled with cracked ice and bottled beer. In turns Susan and I were invited to take the co-pilot's seat, from which the best view is to be had, and how thrilled we were when, having flown through a gorge where it seemed at times as though the plane's wing-tips might touch the trees on either side, we rounded a bend and came suddenly upon the Kaieteur Fall. There the river, which is a tributary of the Essequibo, plunges over a precipice to drop in a torrent of brown and white perpendicularly for 741 ft.; it makes the better known Victoria and Niagara falls with drops respectively of 343 and 167 ft. seem small by comparison.

Most of such flying as Susan and I have done has been in D.C.3s, and we have a high regard for those rugged planes; but the centre of British Guiana struck me as being a particularly inhospitable place, and I asked our pilot, with whom I was sitting at the time, what would become of us if we had to make a forced landing.

'Well,' he said with a grin, 'first you have to find a bit of ground, for those trees aren't quite so soft as they look. Then, if you are still in one piece, you go and look for a river—there are plenty of them—and that will lead you to the coast. The last people who did it took six weeks to get back to Georgetown.'

However, he got us back without having to make use of a river, and for the next three days we were guests of Demba (The Demerara Bauxite Company). Keith Tisshaw, the Public Relations Officer of that huge concern, called for us in a 30-knot motor launch, and took us in great comfort (drinks and lunch served by two stewards) 60 miles up the Demerara River, through the forest and past the lumber camps, to Mackenzie, in the neighbourhood of which bauxite is mined. This town, with a population of about 8,000, lies in a clearing in the forest, and has no roads of approach except the river and the air, yet it has 80 miles of railway connecting it with the workings, from which two million tons of bauxite are exported yearly. We were given a huge cool room in the guest house with fans, iced drinks, and excellent meals—a remarkable contrast to *Wanderer*'s small and overheated cabin—and just outside lay a fine swimming pool. For three nights we remained as pampered guests, and Keith, who we learnt had made the journey entirely on our account, devoted all his time to us; he introduced us in turn to all the managers, and each in person conducted us round his department. We watched the giant dragline removing the over-burden, taking bites of 15 tons a time, staggering forward on its own legs like a man who has not yet grown accustomed to artificial limbs; then came the mechanical shovels to load the ore into rail trucks which carried it to the washing and drying plants at Mackenzie, from which it was loaded into ships. We were also shown something of the social activities, the hospital and the school, where I had to make a speech, most of which was drowned by a downpour of rain beating on the aluminium roof. We began to wonder if some mistake had been made that we should be treated as such V.I.P.s, and I felt embarrassed at my inability to sell any aluminium in return for all this. Their final gesture was to fly us back to Georgetown in a small amphibious plane.

We then sailed *Wanderer* 9 miles up the river and anchored off Wales, one of the larger sugar estates, where the manager, Sammy Cann, of British farming stock, looked after us well, and personally showed us all there is to be seen on an estate em-ploying a thousand people in the production and refining of sugar. He gave us a sack full, and later when we opened it we found concealed among the sugar two silver spoons with the Guianese crest on them.

The weather was beginning to break. The rains were starting, and on one day in showers (if you can rightly call them that) 3 in. fell; the ebb flowed longer and more swiftly, and the mosquitoes became more troublesome. It was time for us to move on, and as we sailed down the river with the first of the ebb on 24 November, out from the fire wharf roared *Lady Woolley*, the largest of the fire-floats, with the Atkinsons on board, to escort us to sea. Playing jets of water against the sky in the form of Prince of Wales' feathers, she gave us a 'fireman's farewell', and as she turned back into the river she made the signal RBA, 'adieu', and dipped her ensign. Quickly the low coastline dropped out of sight astern as we made our way towards the Outer G.T. buoy, which lies 30 miles from the mouth of the river, and which we passed at nightfall.

4

Into the Pacific

When planning a voyage it is, of course, necessary to study the weather in order to take advantage of fair winds and to minimize the risk of encountering calms or gales. Because of the hurricane season, it is not considered wise to arrive in the Caribbean before mid-November, but one may then cruise there in safety until June. However, we had another date to keep with nature in connexion with the passage from Panama to the Galápagos Islands, which lie about a thousand miles out in the Pacific. That passage takes one through an area subject to calms and, in places, contrary currents, and it is wise for a sailing vessel to leave Panama as early in the year as possible, when northerly winds are likely to be encountered, and for preference she should not delay her departure after mid-February. With this in mind we could not afford to spend as much time as we would have liked among the West Indies.

Barbados, the easternmost of the Windward Islands, lies 400 miles north-north-west of Georgetown, and although that was a long way off our course for Panama, we were bound for it because we knew that there we would be allowed to ship the stores out of bond which had been denied us by a disobliging customs official at Georgetown.

After a four-day passage interrupted by squalls and calm patches, we sighted the island in the afternoon, but too far off to be reached before nightfall. We knew that a harbour was under construction there, but as we had no precise information about it or any temporary lights that might be exhibited, and with memories of our nearly disastrous night arrival at St.

Vincent still in mind, we hove-to until daybreak. Then we beat into Carlisle Bay, where we brought up in the well-remembered sparkling, clear water off the Aquatic Club, near several of the yachts we had met in the Canaries, and immediately plunged overboard for our first enjoyable salt-water bathe for many a day.

Lying near us was the 16-ton ketch *Si Ye Pambili*, which means in one of Rhodesia's African languages 'Let's go forward'. She had left England on a world cruise owned and sailed by five Englishmen; all were ex-Rhodesian policemen in their early twenties; but two of them never made the Atlantic crossing, and a third, who had fallen in love with a Spanish girl in the Canaries, left at Barbados. The remaining two, Roger Gowen and Bill Baker, continued the voyage; we were to see more of them and get to know them well when we met again 6,000 miles later at Tahiti.

Two breakwaters were under construction at the north end of Carlisle Bay, but apart from that nothing much had changed in the seven years since our last visit. Our old friend David Payne, one of the port doctors, was off duty, but he had seen *Wanderer* from his house, and at once came out to give us pratique. Ice, drinks, meals, and a friendly welcome awaited us at the red and white striped building of the Aquatic Club, standing on its own pier, which, remarkably, had survived the heavy rollers which now and again had lifted up its lower floor. The Careenage was still packed with inter-island schooners, and Goddards still supplied frosted chocolate on their balcony overlooking the bustling main street, and stores out of bond without the slightest fuss or formality. The same reporter as before came out to get our story, and quiet-spoken Ian Gale still occupied the same editorial chair in the *Advocate* office, and was as hospitable as ever. On this voyage it was our aim to vary our route from the earlier one as much as possible, and since leaving the Tagus, Barbados was the first place to be *re*visited by us; how glad we were to be there again.

With 1,200 miles to go to Panama, we had to hurry on, but we did manage to give the ship a refit at Bequia, and cruised pleasantly down through the Grenadines to Grenada, where we arrived on Christmas Day, and were at once seized by Dr. and Mrs. Slominski (total strangers), who drove us along 14 miles of twisting, exciting roads in the tropic dusk to their home for a real Christmas dinner.

Then we made a smart passage, 430 miles in just under three days, to the Dutch island of Curaçao, where we spent a peaceful night in the small, natural harbour of Spaansche Water before going to the main port of Willemstad. The entrance to that port is spanned by a 500-ft. pontoon bridge, off which we jilled about for more than an hour before we were noticed and the entire bridge hinged at its western end to open a crack and let us in. The place was bustling with activity, as oil from nearby Venezuela is refined on the island and many ships call there for bunkers; the water was coated with oil, and very soon our newly-painted topsides were plastered with the thick, tar-like stuff. It was no place for us, but thanks to the kindness of one of the pilots, we were able to find a safe berth at the windward end of the Schottegat, the small inland sea beyond the town. Apart from phosphate, Curaçao has no natural resources, yet because of its oil refineries it is a prosperous island. Willemstad is a free port, so watches, cameras and jewellery can be bought cheaply there—a tourist attraction which has not been overlooked by the shipping companies—but for all else, including the necessities of life, it is the most expensive place that we have ever visited.

Two nights there were quite enough, after which we hurried on across another 700 miles of very rough Caribbean. The winter trade was by then fully established, and it blew so hard that we were under bare poles for part of the trip and very reduced sail for the remainder, and we were glad to make our usual night arrival at Cristobal/Colon at the north end of the Panama Canal.

Some of the lights and buoys were not as shown on the chart or as given in the *Light List* and *Pilot*, but there was moonlight to help, and as we had been there before we knew where to go; so without much difficulty we reached the anchorage on the flats south of the docks, and when we went on deck at dawn there close beside us was our old friend *Penella*, last met with at Barbados; she had arrived direct from Grenada an hour or two after us. When the business of entering had been completed, and that included the outrageous charge of $13.00 for a quite worthless Deratting Exemption Certificate, we were made welcome at the Panama Canal Yacht Club, and were given a comfortable and convenient berth alongside one of its piers, so convenient indeed that we dined most evenings during our stay at the Club, where the superb 'sizzling' steaks ringed with rashers of smoky bacon really did make that appetizing noise as they were hurried to the table on the dishes in which they had been cooked. There we embarked a couple of un-welcome visitors in the form of cockroaches; they came to us from the pages of the Club visitors' book, which we were unwise enough to take on board. I think we were fortunate to have no rats, for when it rains hard in Colon we have seen large ones come out of the drains and stroll about the streets.

Knowing something of the dangers attending a small yacht's transit of the Canal, I arranged with Traffic Control for *Wanderer* to have a centre lockage in the three up-locks at Gatun; a pilot was to board us at 6 a.m., for pilotage is compulsory, and Leigh and Dorrie Rankin from *Penella* kindly agreed to come with us through the up-locks to handle two of our four 100-ft. lines. But nothing went according to plan. Our pilot had received instructions to come aboard at 9 a.m. instead of 6 a.m., but nobody had bothered to tell us of the change of plan, and when we reached the Gatun approach we were too early and had to jill about for an hour in a very strong wind, waiting for a succession of ships to go ahead of us. Eventually we entered the first lock astern of the British freighter *Northumberland*. Steel-helmeted lock hands were standing by to send us heaving lines so that we could, as arranged, secure ourselves in the centre of the chamber, where we could come to no harm when the inrush of water began; but to our dismay the lock master refused us the centre lockage and ordered us to secure alongside a canal tug which was then entering. That was just the situation we had planned to avoid, so, of course, we had only our normal yacht fenders, which are of little use against a tug with a massive rubbing strake. However, there was no alternative, so we did as we were told, a difficult manoeuvre with water running out of the lock and the wind blowing straight in to it, for like most sailing yachts with low-powered engines and small propellers, *Wanderer* will not handle properly when astern gear is engaged, and she made a shocking exhibition of herself. The tug had some good coir fenders, but her skipper refused to lower them to a position where they could have been of use to us. The gates closed, the water boiled as it lifted us up 27 ft., *Wanderer* tugged at her lines and heeled over, and the five of us, for the pilot lent a hand too, struggled to hold fenders in place and prevent damage. When the tumult subsided the tug dragged us into the next lock, where the process was repeated, and then into the third lock. How thankful we were when at last, 80 ft. above the ocean, we were free to cast off and proceed on our own out on to the broad waters of Gatun Lake. We landed the Rankins, who had been so helpful, motored through narrow Banana Cut, which saves a mile or two, then set sail and got moving properly under full control for the first time that day. Our pilot, a pleasant American who had been in the Zone for only six months, and had never before handled a sailing craft, appeared to enjoy himself, raising his white topee and waving to his fellow pilots in passing ships. On we sped among the jungle-clad islands, past the many buoys marking the big ship channel, and into Gaillard Cut, which was in the process of being widened; there sailing is forbidden, so we had to continue under power, meeting a stream of ships going the other way, to the first of the down-locks at Pedro Miguel (Peter MacGill the Americans call it). We had to wait there for *Northumberland* to catch up with us; she had been held up in Gatun Lake, waiting for a large tanker to go through. Some of these new tankers are so long and inconveniently arranged that they carry five pilots during the transit; we were told that aboard those which have the bridge aft the officer on watch can see nothing on the water ahead nearer than 8 miles. We shared all three down-locks with *Northumberland*, and lay comfortably alongside a banana boat, which had plenty of nice fat fenders; but going down presents no serious problem, for the water subsides quite gently. However, the speed at which our pilot took us into those locks terrified us. With the motor running full ahead, the wind, still fresh, pushing us in, and the current going that way also, the lamp-posts flicked swiftly by, and the great protective chain and gates at the far end approached with awful speed. Of course, we had to rely entirely on going astern to check our headlong career, and naturally the pilot, who called this manoeuvre 'beating the current', could not be expected to appreciate the fact that one small piece of fluff or a drop of water in the carburettor jet at the crucial moment could have spelt finish to our voyage.

Night had fallen by the time the last pair of gates opened ponderously ahead and the chain dropped to let us out into the Pacific Ocean. A message had been sent ahead from the last lock, and a boatman was waiting to show us to a mooring when we arrived off the Balboa Yacht Club. The transit of 40 miles had taken 11 hours.

Balboa is no longer the good place it used to be for provisioning a yacht for a long voyage. Since the Suez trouble the Panamanians have got ideas about canals. One result of this is that the Americans, who run an excellent commissary at Balboa for the use of people employed by the canal company, have agreed not to allow visiting yachts to purchase anything there, thus forcing them to make the tiresome bus journey into Panama City, where prices are higher and quality is poor. However, we were most fortunate in being looked after by a friendly young American couple who were greatly interested in ocean voyaging. They bought for us everything we required on their own cards at the commissary—thereby taking a risk, for that is a punishable offence—so when we left the Canal Zone on 4 February bound for the Galápagos Islands and then on across the Pacific, we lacked nothing.

As I have said, the passage to the Galápagos Islands, which straddle the Equator 1,000 miles south-west of Panama, is not

an easy one for a sailing vessel, but we did not manage too
badly. For the first two days there was complete calm, so we
motored 10 miles to the island of Taboga and remained there
until a breeze made. It was fair and lasted for three days, but
thereafter we mostly had light headwinds, and it became a
constant struggle to make the southing which is so essential to
avoid being set by the current into an area north of the islands
where the percentage of calm is very high. However, *Wanderer*
obligingly steered herself for much of the time, so that we were
able to get all the sleep we needed; the sea was remarkably
smooth, though occasionally, and particularly in the neighbourhood of Malpelo—a barren, inaccessible rock some 300
miles out from Panama—we passed through swirls and hissing
ripples which had every appearance of tide races or overfalls.

During the forenoon of our twelfth day at sea we were
equidistant, 35 miles, from the anchorages at Hood Island and
Chatham Island. We thought it wise to go to Chatham, because the little port there, known as Wreck Bay, is the official
port of entry, and we had with us the necessary papers which
we had obtained for a small charge from the Ecuadorean
Consul at Colon. But that day the course to Wreck Bay was a
dead run, whereas that to uninhabited Hood Island was a
reach, and therefore faster sailing to give us a good chance of
arriving before nightfall; so we headed that way, and in the
afternoon anchored in the roadstead off the island's northern
shore. It was a rolly berth, and the swell breaking on the beach
did not encourage us to attempt a landing.

On a previous voyage we had found that British charts of
many of the Pacific islands are indifferent or even poor. Of the
Galápagos Islands, fourteen in number, extending over 2 deg.
of latitude and 2½ deg. of longitude, there is only one small
sheet with a scale of 10 miles to the inch, and with a few indifferent plans inset. However, the archipelago is very well
covered by more than a dozen large-scale American charts,
which our friends at Balboa had kindly lent to us; on them they
had written scraps of useful information, for they had spent
some time out there in their own yacht: 'Dig here for treasure'

—'Iguanas and turtles abound'—'Port Captain a dirty guy'—
'Penguin rookery'—'A lousy anchorage', and the like. I think
one might describe most of the anchorages among those islands
as 'lousy', for practically all of them are open to a large expanse
of ocean. Nevertheless I would recommend any yacht voyaging
out into the Pacific to call at at least one of those remarkable
islands where all manner of creatures can be seen in their
natural setting.

Originally the islands had British names, the first survey
being made by H.M.S. *Beagle* in 1836, but now each has a
Spanish name as well. Either may be used, and to avoid confusion I will give both when referring to the islands here.

After one uncomfortable night at Hood (Española) Island,
we sailed 30 miles across to Chatham (San Cristobal) Island,
and worked our way in among the reefs which give the place
some protection from the north-west, to an anchorage in Wreck
Bay, where we brought up shortly after noon. At 1.55 p.m. a
boat put out to us from the shore bearing the Commandant (a
naval officer), three other officials, and an interpreter; the latter
was the brother-in-law of the Ecuadorean Ambassador in
Paris, and was then serving his time in the Navy, a pleasant,
well-mannered young man; the rest were a bit surly. They took
our papers ashore, and when we went to collect them next day,
Saturday, before sailing, we discovered that the Ecuadorean
Navy has learnt the useful word 'overtime'. Through the interpreter the gross Commandant—who failed to rise from the
rocking-chair behind his desk when Susan entered his office—
told us that as he had come out to grant pratique at 1.55 p.m.
instead of waiting until 2 o'clock (the end of the lunch hour) we
would have to pay $10.00 for 'overtime'. He also said that if
we left that afternoon, or any time on Sunday, or before 8 a.m.
on Monday, there would be another $10.00 to pay, although
the office work had been done and our papers returned to us.
I told the interpreter to tell the Commandant exactly what I
thought of him, but I don't think he did, for the fat man continued to rock in his chair unruffled. The temptation to leave
when we wished and without paying was considerable, but we

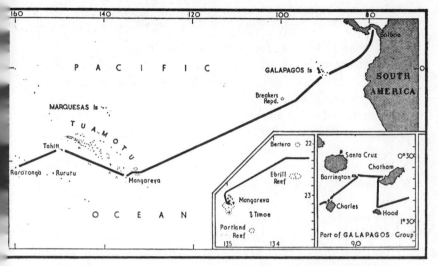

EASTERN PART OF SOUTH PACIFIC, WITH INSETS
SHOWING PART OF GALAPAGOS GROUP AND APPROACHES
TO MANGAREVA

resisted it, because there was a rusty but mobile gunboat in the port, which no doubt the Commandant would have been delighted to send after us to earn a bit more 'overtime'. Fortunately we had with us, and flew on arrival, an Ecuadorean ensign, because failure to do that is punished by a fine of $15.00. In one of his delightful books Irving Johnson has written that Ecuador is the most backward country of all. He should know, for he has made seven circumnavigations of the globe in his two *Yankees*, but I feel that Ecuador is coming on.

The settlement of Wreck Bay, a litter of timber shacks scattered along the sand beach, with a rickety jetty bearing an enormous water pipe, the contents of which are unfit for drinking, had little of interest or entertainment to offer us, and after a tiresome wait we left at 8 o'clock precisely on Monday morning. The delay cost us dear. During Saturday afternoon and all Sunday a fine wind blew to waste, but Monday dawned calm and remained so, and much of our small fuel supply was expended in getting to Barrington (Santa Fé) Island before dark.

Barrington, 5 miles long, 3 miles wide, and rising to a height of 860 ft., is uninhabited, and at its north-east corner lies the best and most sheltered anchorage in the group. There is no chart of that little harbour, which is protected on its south and west sides by the island, and on its north side by a long reef, most of which is awash at high water, with an islet at its extremity. It is easy of access if one approaches from the north-east and borrows a little on the islet side. This is the place I would recommend any yacht to visit if her people cannot be bothered with the tedious and expensive business of getting entered at Wreck Bay, for here can be seen at close quarters a fine selection of Galápagos wild life in its natural setting, and one is unlikely to be disturbed.

We entered in the late afternoon with the sun ahead of us, but the water was so clear that we had no difficulty in avoiding the shoal patches and finding a good anchorage in 2 fathoms on a clean sand bottom.

Both sides of the harbour are of black rock on which we found large numbers of scarlet crabs and black sea-iguanas. At the western end, separated by a spur of low rock, are two sand beaches, on one of which no fewer than thirty sealions were sleeping or basking. When we landed and walked among them, most that we disturbed just gave a snort and turned over on the other side to resume their slumbers; but a few dragged themselves with their flippers awkwardly down the beach, and the moment they entered the sea appeared to become different creatures—the speed and grace of their swimming was lovely to watch as they glided effortlessly about and then stood, so it seemed, on their tails, looking curiously at us, their bodies sleek and glossy. 'How they love it,' remarked Susan; 'they're proper waterbabies.' Only the old, war-scarred bulls objected to us. Roaring angrily, one or two of them even went so far as to flounder clumsily towards us, presumably in an attempt to drive us off the beach; but on the sand they cannot move very fast. However, I nearly capsized the dinghy with laughter when on another occasion I was trying to film Susan as she retreated cautiously before a belligerent old bull; but my amusement quickly turned to dismay when he suddenly left her and launched a lightning-like attack on the dinghy in which I had all our photographic equipment.

There were a great many turtles, and from up *Wanderer*'s mast we could often count a dozen or more as they paddled slowly about the little harbour; but they were the only timid inhabitants, and did not often come close. Also there were sting-rays, sinister aces of spades, digging in the sand beneath our clearly visible anchor chain; and huge shoals of bright green fish, swimming in tight formation near the surface with their mouths wide open—'when mother says turn, we all turn'. A party of puffer fish took up their station underneath *Wanderer* shortly after her arrival, and soon became so tame that they took food from Susan's fingers, and popped out to investigate anything we threw overboard.

On the rocks among the crabs and iguanas stood pelicans, surely the most delightfully absurd and likeable of birds, their huge beaks resting on their breasts, benign expressions on their faces. The take-off of so large a bird is spectacular, but on approaching with the movie camera we had great difficulty in making them fly; when one or other of us got within prodding distance, our pelican stepped on to the next rock and went to sleep again. To make a landing on the water, these birds simply stop in mid air and fall with a tremendous splash.

Barrington is not much of an island on which to take a walk, for its surface is composed almost entirely of volcanic debris and loose boulders, and if you slip and stretch out to the vegetation to steady yourself, you end up with a handful of spines from the cacti, which are almost the only plants to flourish there. Yet our scrambles ashore were rewarding. The birds were so tame that they followed us about, waiting for a stone to be turned over so that they might grab any worms or insects brought to light, and there was always a chance of coming upon a land iguana sunning itself. Imagine the dragon of the fairy tales; scale him down to about 4 ft. in length, and you have the Galapagos land iguana. His golden body covered with scales, a spiny ridge running down his back; a big mouth from which you almost expect to see flames lick out, large round eyes staring balefully—he certainly is a frightening creature to encounter at close quarters for the first time. But like most of the other inhabitants of that island, the land iguana is harmless, and so unafraid of man that one can get within a few feet of him.

A remarkable thing about the little harbour at Barrington is that it appears by common consent to be a sanctuary. Never once did we see there any creature attacking or molesting another, yet the daily fish intake of a sealion, bigger than a man, must be prodigious, and the pelican has no mean appetite.

By night the sounds were magnified, for usually the wind died right away then. The surge sucked wetly at the rocks and broke with a hiss on the beaches; there were noises almost of human origin from the sealions: grunts, snores, and coughs, and the occasional bellow of a bull.

The visit to Barrington was one of our strangest and most enjoyable experiences, and even when we left long before dawn of our fifth night there, Barrington life put on a farewell show. As we passed out through the entrance, around and beneath us were patches and streaks of pale green phosphorescent light, where fish and other creatures moved about their business. Then a party of porpoises, swift, inter-weaving, luminous torpedoes, joined company with us, and joyfully swimming close ahead, escorted us down the island's eastern side.

During the forty-mile crossing to Post Office Bay on Charles (Floriana) Island the compass was useless, because of abnormal magnetic variation, and the current, which set south-west instead of north-west as shown on the chart, was strong. No wonder the Galápagos were known to the early navigators as the Enchanted Islands; one day an island would appear, and the next, due to current or compass error, there might be no sign of land. Indeed, in the past some voyages have been made from ports in South America towards the Galápagos from which

PLATE 7
The Kaieteur Fall, where a tributary of British Guiana's Essequibo River plunges vertically for 741 ft. in a torrent of brown and white.

the ships returned without having been able to find a trace of the islands. Fortunately for us visibility was good that day, and for most of the trip we had four islands in sight at the same time.

We anchored in Post Office Bay, which is on the north side of Charles Island, in the afternoon, and at once landed to have a look at the famous post office barrel, in which outward bound whalers used to place their mail to be collected by the home-ward-bounders—a tradition which is carried on today only by the occasional yacht or tuna fishing vessel calling there. The barrel, which had been repaired and painted by *Yankee*'s crew a few years before, was festooned with the names of yachts, some famous ones among them—*Yankee*, *Arthur Rogers*, *Tzu Hang*, *Salmo* and *Solace*—and we added *Wanderer*'s which Susan painted in modestly small letters on a piece of iroko. Then we photographed ourselves standing alongside it, developed the film and put a negative in an envelope addressed to the Editor of *Yachting World* (that magazine was serializing our story, and so helping to make the voyage a financial possibility). We put the envelope in a plastic bag together with a few shillings to pay postage, and wondered how long it would take, and by what route, to reach its destination. Since then three years have passed, and it has not arrived, so either there has not been another visitor, which is hard to believe, or more probably the ants have eaten it, plastic bag and all.

Next day we sailed round to the island's western side to spend a night off Black Beach, an uneasy anchorage where the swell broke angrily on the rocks and the sand. We went there to call on the Wittmers, a German family who settled there thirty years ago, and have successfully wrested a living from the island ever since. The son, Rolf, was occupying himself with the dry-fish business in preparation for the Lent market in Ecuador. His method, which surely must be unique, was to shoot a fish from his boat and then dive in to retrieve it before it sank. They

PLATE 8
The wild life at Barrington Island, Galápagos, was quite unafraid of us. *Top:* A scarlet crab. *Bottom:* A young sealion.

B.W.H.—E

gave us lunch, and we were able to buy a few things from them, including some excellent fresh-baked bread, before taking our departure for Mangareva, 3,000 miles away to the west-south-west. We would have liked to remain longer among the Galápagos Islands and to have visited more of them, but we had to consider the long voyage ahead, and provisions and good water are hard to come by there. Also we were there at a time of year when calms and light airs prevail, and our small petrol supply, which the Commandant had not permitted us to replenish at Wreck Bay, was almost finished.

5

Three Thousand Miles
to the Far Mountain

From Panama or from the Galápagos Islands the usual route taken by yachts bound for Tahiti is by way of the Marquesas, which lie in about 9° south latitude; but we, wishing to visit a less frequented place, were bound towards the island of Mangareva, down in the south-east corner of Oceania, in 25° south latitude, and near the edge of the trade-wind belt. The furrow to Mangareva has not been ploughed very often, and then only by the occasional yacht, perhaps one in every ten or twelve years; it passes through just about as empty a stretch of ocean as one could find, and it would be the longest passage we should have to make during this circumnavigation. Once we had left the neighbourhood of Galápagos, all of it should lie within the region of the south-east trade wind; but as the course has so much southing in it, we knew that the wind would often be too much abeam to permit the twin self-steering sails to work, and that we would therefore have to spend a lot of time at the helm. On the pilot charts, which show the strength and direction of wind and the percentages of calms and gales that have been experienced in the area covered over a period of many years, there were several five degree squares through which we had to pass where the average strength of the south-east wind was given as force 5 on the Beaufort scale, a fresh breeze. Indeed, when we had left the islands a few hundred miles astern the beam wind was so boisterous for several days that life aboard became most unpleasant and we both felt squeamish and unable to eat much. The ship was thrown so violently to leeward that proper rest was not possible, and there were times when we were tempted to bear away and run more easily for the Marquesas.

It was during the early part of the trip that a nagging pain in the appropriate part of my abdomen, between navel and hip bone, suggested to me that I was developing appendicitis. Miserably I realized that there was nothing to be done, for it would have been a long, slow and rough business sailing back to Galápagos, and there was no doctor on those islands. There was no point in telling Susan about my symptoms, but after a day or two I could no longer keep the horrid secret to myself.

'I've got a pain in my tummy,' I said eventually, 'and I think it may be appendicitis.'

Susan did not appear to be as concerned as I thought she would be, and after I had pinpointed the spot she said:

'Well, I've had a pain there, too, for the past few days, and it can't possibly be appendicitis in my case, as I've had mine out.'

I felt tremendously relieved, and the final conclusion we came to was that it must be some form of poisoning, possibly due to Wreck Bay water, even though we had boiled it, and slowly we both recovered.

For the first few days out from Black Beach we did not steer direct for Mangareva, because we wished to pass well clear of our first Pacific vigia, one of those dangers of doubtful position and uncertain existence in which this ocean abounds, and which are the bane of navigators, for one can never be sure where they are, if they are there at all. On the chart this one was shown as a small dotted circle, and alongside it the words: 'Breakers and discoloured water reported 1906 and 1925.' We passed to the south of it, giving it a berth of about 50 miles, and then altered course a little more westerly direct for Mangareva.

PLATE 9
We felt insignificant mites as we forged our way across the vast, blue, empty spaces of the Pacific, watching the momentary impression of our wake being wiped out a few yards astern to leave no trace of our passing.

As we progressed the wind eased a little and drew more aft, and from then on the greater part of that long passage, during which we saw no ships or aircraft, only a few flying fish, and remarkably few birds, turned out to be quite enjoyable, and we even got the ship to steer herself under the twin spinnakers at times. The Pacific is the greatest of the oceans, with an area of 63,000,000 sq. miles, and we felt insignificant mites as we forged our way across its vast blue and rolling spaces, watching the slight momentary impression of our wake being wiped out a few yards astern to leave no trace of our passing.

Each morning two or three hours before noon I took an observation of the sun, Susan checking with a stopwatch the time that elapsed between the taking of the sight and the reading of the chronometer. The latter we were able to check most evenings with time signals from the American radio station WWVH, which is situated in the Hawaiian Islands and gives the time every five minutes throughout the day. Mostly the chronometer kept a steady losing rate of two seconds a day; the only thing to upset it was a sudden change of temperature, but that only occurred outside the tropics. For working the sight I used the clearly printed *Astronomical Navigation Tables*. These are no longer published, and have been replaced by *Sight Reduction Tables for Air Navigation*, which are just as easy to use, but are not so boldly printed. At noon I obtained a meridian altitude sight, and where the first position line, brought forward along the course steered for the number of miles we had sailed since getting it, crossed the noon latitude was assumed to be our noon position; but, of course, bad steering or a current between the taking of the sights could affect it slightly. This drawing I did on a Baker's position line chart, and then transferred the position to the Pacific Ocean general chart, which is the only one available showing both our point of departure and our destination on the same sheet. Because of the small scale, about

PLATE 10
Becalmed 800 miles from the nearest land, *Wanderer* looked curiously frail and vulnerable out there alone on the silent, slowly heaving ocean beneath an immensity of sky.

300 miles to the inch in our latitude, the crosses were very.close together, but most were equidistant; these were the measure of our progress.

The futility of man's attempts to tie nature down to a set of rules, or to show that she arranges things in percentages or obeys the law of averages, was impressed once more upon us during this long passage. When we had reached a point midway between Galápagos and Mangareva, with the nearest land, Easter Island, 800 miles away to the south, and were in a five degree square where the pilot chart showed 52 per cent of south-east wind and 48 per cent of east wind, and no calms, the wind fell lighter and lighter; the bow wave, which had roared day and night without a pause for the past 1,500 miles, dropped to a chuckle as our speed slackened, and finally died away as *Wanderer*, quite becalmed, stood upright above her own reflection. The sea changed from wind-ruffled dark blue to a colour so matching the sky that one could scarcely see the boundary between them, and the stationary clouds were mirrored in it. Apart from the listless flapping of the idle nylon spinnakers, the silence was profound. There was some swell, of course, for the open oceans are never quite free from that, but it was longer and lower than usual, a gentle undulation; so we were able to launch the dinghy in order that I might row away to see what our small ship looked like becalmed in an empty ocean, something neither of us had ever done before.

At sea I do not think either of us is normally conscious of the smallness of our ship, or suffers from a feeling of loneliness. There is nothing to scale her by; she is sturdy and compact, the centre of our universe for the time being; we have each other for company, and our time is fully occupied. But when I had rowed a hundred yards or so away from *Wanderer*, I began to realize how small she was; she looked curiously frail and vulnerable, and very beautiful, out there on the silent, slowly heaving ocean beneath an immensity of sky. Her smallness was emphasized by the length of time her hull was hidden from my view by the intervening swell, and the peculiar angles she assumed when she did come into sight, for there was no straight or steady line anywhere on which to fix my eye. Having taken my photographs, I remembered that the sea on which I was floating in my cockleshell dinghy was more than two miles deep, and although one can drown just as easily in six feet of water as in two miles of it, I suddenly felt scared of I don't know what, and rowed back to *Wanderer* rather faster than I had rowed away. As Susan grabbed the dinghy painter she said:

'I'm glad you are back. We don't seem to have been so far away from one another since we left home.'

The calm lasted twenty-four hours, long enough to give us a rest, but not long enough for us to imagine it would last indefinitely, which is our usual reaction to calms and gales, or to allow us to get bored. Early next morning there were patches where the sea, ruffled by a faint air, was of a darker colour, and we could feel a coolness on our faces. The sails began to fill, the masthead flag stopped swivelling aimlessly on its stick and pointed a direction; the dark patches amalgamated as the gentle south-east breeze became more general, and within the hour *Wanderer* was bustling on her way, her bow-wave roaring merrily as she settled down in her trade-wind stride.

From that point on the passage continued uneventfully, as all good trade-wind passages should, and day followed day of perfect weather. Each morning the sun rose brilliantly in the east, and we had to spread the small awning to keep his blinding rays out of the cabin; he scorched the deck at his zenith, passed clean overhead on 20 March (I had to face north instead of south thereafter when taking the noon sight); he was only hidden occasionally for a moment or two when a neat little cloud covered his face, and in the evening he usually sank into a soft bank of grey, fine-weather cloud. Then overhead Orion materialized and to port the Southern Cross; we took some star sights for practice, as we might need their help when making a landfall, and all too soon the horizon had gone and the tropic night of twelve hours' duration was upon us. When steering was necessary we divided the night after supper so as to take two watches each, and always took the same ones, finding that more restful than changing the routine each night. Susan took the first one, from 9 till 11.30 p.m., and when she called me to take over I was usually far gone in sleep, but the familiar 'Darling, give me a spell-O', repeated once perhaps, broke through the barriers of sleep. Lifting myself over the canvas bunkboard, I pulled on a short-sleeved shirt and a pair of nylon beach shorts, all the clothes I needed those tropic nights, took a couple of biscuits from the tin on the galley bench, and changed places with Susan, sitting on the warm patch that she had left behind her, my bare feet gripping the cockpit grating. As this passage occupied a lunar month, we had the moon in every phase; but she was not yet up, so I could only see Susan dimly down in the cabin as she pulled her shirt over her head and slipped into her bunk; it was hot in the cabin, and one needed no covering.

The first part of the watch was a pleasure, and I enjoyed our ship's easy, buoyant progress over the heaving ocean, and the lively feel of the tiller in my hand. The brush of the wind sweeping in over the top of the weathercloths, rigged on the guardrails each side of the cockpit, was almost a caress, and my body was no longer damp with sweat. I thought idly of many things; of the wild life at Santa Fé; of the Wittmer family at Black Beach; and I wondered what Mangareva (that beautiful name means 'The Far Mountain') would be like. But chiefly I thought, in a dreamy kind of way, of how very fortunate I was to be out here with Susan as my companion making this long voyage. It would be 8 a.m. in England now, and in other circumstances I might be there in some dreary suburb, having my breakfast preparatory to spending the day in an insurance office or a bank, and with nothing new to look forward to tomorrow and tomorrow. The wretchedness of this thought must have woken me up, for I realized that *Wanderer* was far off her course with the spinnaker lifting. I put her back to west-south-west, and slipping a line round the tiller, stood up and looked all round; then with a hand each side of the hatchway, I leant over the bridge deck and put my head into the cabin. A shaft of silver light from the newly risen moon (we call this a lunarbell) was looking in through one of the ports, darting to and fro as *Wanderer* rolled, and now and then it crossed Susan's face. With her cheek resting on her hand and her head moving a little to the motion, she looked touchingly helpless and trustful as she slept. But that lunarbell would wake her in a moment; so I checked the course, tightened the tiller line a trifle, and tiptoeing down the steps quickly fitted a lunartrap (a piece of cardboard secured to a rubber suction cup) over the port to shut it out, and got back to the helm before *Wanderer* knew anything about it.

In fact, she seemed to be doing nicely without any attention from me, so I lay down on the lee cockpit seat with my head pillowed on the slightly raised bridge deck so that I could keep an eye on the compass, but now and then I had to give the tiller a gentle push. If I lay on my back I could watch the stars swinging dizzily overhead, and I got out the binoculars from the shelf beside the compass to have a closer look. What a tremendous lot of them there were; how cold and infinitely distant they looked! Even my old friend Sirius, the brightest of them all, seemed aloof just then—perhaps disapproving of my method of keeping watch. If *Wanderer* sprang an uncontrollable leak and went down like a stone, as indeed she would with three-and-a-half tons of lead ballast clinging to her keel, those stars would continue to stare coldly and unwinkingly down for countless millions of years. I felt very small and unimportant.

It is said that as one grows older one needs less sleep, but I find this is not so. On this voyage I found it more difficult to keep awake during the night watches than ever I had done before, and the last half-hour was painful with the struggle to keep my eyes open. I did all the things I could think of to keep awake. I shook my head vigorously from side to side; I stood up and examined carefully every inch of the empty horizon; I counted in the heavens all the stars I knew by name; I shone the beam from a torch on the dial of the spinning patent log and noted that we had sailed twelve miles in the past two hours; and I ate some chocolate. In that final half-hour I must have looked at my watch fifty times; it seemed to have stopped. But eventually the hands crept round to 2 o'clock, and with relief that my trick was over, but sorry to have to call Susan, who was so soundly asleep, I went below and put a hand on her shoulder, calling her name. She stirred, opened an eye, and instantly sat up. 'Coming,' she said, and returning to the cockpit I had to wait only a few moments before she was with me, yawning widely.

'No lights, no nothing; but Sirius is over the lower crosstrees.'

How welcoming my frowsty bunk felt as I slid into it and stuffed a cushion between my back and the bunkboard; but I scarcely seemed to have been in it a minute when I heard Susan's voice calling me, and knew I must go on deck again to stand the morning watch, and keep awake till dawn.

So the routine continued, watch and watch night after night, except on those blessed but too rare occasions when the ship agreed to steer herself, and then we had the luxury of all night in our bunks.

Our runs on this passage were not spectacular, and we had little current to help us over the last 2,000 miles. The first week of the trip we made good 742 miles, the best day's run being 146, and we never bettered that. The second week out our total was 792; the third was very poor with a total of only 553, and the fourth week 704.

The approach to Mangareva from the east or north-east is beset with certain difficulties. Twenty miles east of the island lies Timoe, an uninhabited atoll, and south of that atoll lies Portland Reef with a least depth of 4½ fathoms, on which the sea is said to break heavily even in quiet weather. These did not concern us, as we had decided to make our approach more directly from the east-north-east. But on that route lie two vigias, one known as Ebrill Reef, and the other, 25 miles north of it, as Bertero. The ship *Sir George Grey* is believed to have been lost on Ebrill in 1865, the reef then being reported to lie about 80 miles east-north-east of Mangareva. A report in 1872 stated that it consisted of a large bank ringed with motus, and it is so marked on the latest chart. But in 1880 search was made for it by H.M.S. *Alert*, and no sign of it was found. Two years later, however, the German barque *Erato* passed over a shoal a few miles south-west of the charted position of Ebrill, and the reef was again seen in 1922 close to that position, when it was said to be breaking heavily in a smooth sea. We therefore felt almost certain that Ebrill Reef did not lie in the position given to it on the chart. Of Bertero we had no information beyond the fact that it is shown on the chart of 1955 corrected to 1959, but not on earlier charts. It would therefore appear to be a recent discovery, but *Pacific Islands Pilot*, Vol. III, does not mention it. We have since learnt that the French Navy has made an unsuccessful search for Ebrill Reef, but we have failed to meet anyone in the islands who has ever heard of Bertero.

We made it our business to pass midway between these two vigias, and it certainly was an eerie sensation after being out of sight of land for twenty-eight days, and navigating solely by sun and stars, to pass between two charted dangers of which we saw nothing. I must admit that the windy night we spent in their vicinity, our eyes and ears strained to detect the first sign of breakers, was not pleasant, and as there were whitecaps everywhere it was unlikely that we could have seen or heard breakers in time to avoid them.

Mangareva is the largest of ten little islands, being five miles long and half a mile wide at its narrowest. The lagoon in which these islands lie is enclosed by a coral reef, which is awash and continuous on the north and east sides, but has considerable depths over it elsewhere. On the reef stand many motus, narrow, often palm-clad islands rising only a few feet above sea level. All the islands within the lagoon have jaunty little peaks, that of Mangareva, known as Mount Duff, rising steeply to a height of 1,440 ft.

Dawn of our twenty-ninth day at sea was different from its predecessors. There were many heavy black clouds about, and a particularly sinister-looking one to the south-west, where we hoped the islands lay; standing vertically against that sombre background were the vivid colours of a broad, short rainbow. The glass, contrary to its usual movements in trade-wind areas, was falling steadily. At 8 a.m. Susan got a bearing of a peak which we took to be Mount Duff, but almost at once heavy rain came pouring down to obscure it. We held our course, often being unable to see more than a few ship's lengths through the downpour, and when two hours later the rain cleared, we found that an unsuspected east-running current had put us uncomfortably close to the barrier reef. We altered course to skirt its northern edge, and in the afternoon entered the lagoon by way of the western pass, which is deep and straightforward. A small choppy sea was running in the lagoon, which is 15 miles square, and it took us some time to make our way round the south coast of Mangareva towards the village of Rikitea, which lies on the eastern side, and where it was our intention to bring up. But the deep pool off the village is hemmed in by a network of coral reefs—it is these which protect it so well from the prevailing east and south-east winds—and the channel through is difficult. By then the sun was getting low, and even from up aloft it was not easy to pick a way through the reefs. But we had been seen from the shore, and soon a boat came out bringing the Gendarme who administers the islands. Quickly and efficiently he piloted us in, and we secured alongside the miniature grass-grown wharf off the village, where a party of laughing islanders had gathered to see the new arrivals, for Mangareva only gets a schooner from Tahiti (900 miles away) once every three months, and a visit from a strange and un-expected ship is quite an occasion.

The Gendarme did not ask us to fill in any forms, but he told us that as Mangareva is not a port of entry we might remain there for two nights only, and must then go straight on to Tahiti.

Susan pleaded with him. 'We have come a long, long way to see your island,' she said, 'and we are very tired.'

'I will radio M. le Gouverneur,' was all that he would say.

As so often happens, it is the first evening in port after a long time at sea that remains most firmly in one's memory. As the sun dropped behind Mount Duff and the cool of the evening

---

PLATE II
Noéline was sitting between Roger Gowen (on the right) and Bill Baker aboard *Pambili* when I asked her to dance the *tamure*. She rehearsed painstakingly and performed enchantingly. (These shots are from our 16 mm. movie film.)

enveloped us, we experienced a feeling of content and peace. Slowly we made our way about the strangely steady deck, giving the sails a harbour stow and tidying up the gear, and off from the land stole the scent of flowers, copra, and wood smoke, the unforgettable and nostalgic scents of Polynesia. After we had eaten our evening meal and were washing up, we heard voices and the tuning twang of guitars, and looking out we found a party of islanders sitting on the edge of the wharf, their bare feet on *Wanderer*'s salt-rimed rail. Quietly and slowly at first, then with increasing volume and tempo, they played and sang for us. Melody followed melody as the sickle of the young moon followed the sun over the mountain, and as everyone wore behind his ear a white bloom of *tiare Tahiti*, the still air was rich with sweet perfume.

Next day we were enjoying the luxury of our first freshwater wash for a long time in the Gendarme's shower, which, as he had pointed out, was *tres moderne*—a curved sheet of corrugated iron arranged vertically, and overhead a 44-gallon oil drum of water—when he rattled on the iron with his cane and shouted:

'M. Isscock, it is all right. Le Gouverneur he say you can stay for two weeks.'

Later, and I think after he had kept an eye on us and approved our behaviour, he told us over a rum-punch on the veranda of his house that there was no limit imposed, and that the Governor of French Oceania had said we could remain and enjoy Mangareva for as long as we wished.

In these sophisticated days it is a wonderful experience to call at a place which is so far off the beaten track that the islanders can remember only one British yacht having called there before, the *Arthur Rogers*, since turned trader. It is so difficult to reach by normal means that visitors are very rare. The islanders seem happy and unspoilt. They have no motor vehicles of any kind, no radio sets (except the Government one),

PLATE 12

Top: In coral waters pilotage is best done by eye from up aloft, provided the sun is high and not ahead. *Bottom:* At Taapuna we spent many hours in the dinghy, drifting over the colourful mysteries of the reef.

and no gramophones. They make their own entertainment, and each evening of our stay a party came out along the wharf to sing for us, just as they had on the first night. We made tape-recordings of some of their songs, and when we played the first one back there was a moment of silent amazement, followed by that most satisfying Polynesian exclamation of delight, a long-drawn-out '*Ei-eee*', and then a roar of laughter. But the novelty soon wore off, and we realized that they preferred singing to listening.

Their island is beautiful. The strip of flat land near the water's edge is luxuriously covered with palms, bananas, and a wealth of other shady trees, under which the dwellings nestle. From our berth few of the buildings were visible, but we could see rearing up above the tree-tops the twin white towers of the huge church built by the fanatical priest Laval, who virtually enslaved the islanders for some years and caused the death of many of them; and here and there among the greenery catch a glimpse of a bright red roof, or a neat little privy standing on stilts in the water. Behind the trees Mount Duff stood sharp against the sky.

The people were most generous and hospitable, and expected nothing in return, for they regarded us as their guests. Each day gifts of chicken, fish, limes, bananas, oranges, and paw-paw were brought in such quantities that we scarcely knew how to deal with them. Of course, we gave some small thing in return —fish-hooks, soap, cigarettes, or whatever we discovered the people lacked—but as we had been out of reach of a shop for nearly three months, *Wanderer*'s lockers were growing empty, and we were unable to make the kind of return we would have wished.

One man, hearing of our arrival, walked over the hill from his village at the far side of the island to bring us gifts, and to introduce us to his sister, the attractive young schoolmistress, who took away all our dirty laundry and returned it crisp and spotless. Another couple had us to their shady home on the edge of the beach for lunch: *poisson cru* (raw fish steeped in the juice of fresh limes and served with coconut cream); *langouste* (the husband had spent the previous night out on the reef catching this, for lobsters are rare); *poule à la casserole*, and an excellent fruit salad. On another occasion we were taken by canoe to a neighbouring island, Akamaru, where a sack of oranges was gathered and given to us, and we had a picnic lunch of fresh-caught fish cooked on a fire of coconut husks and eaten in the shade of the palms. Everybody knew us and seemed to take an interest in us, and as we strolled along the half-mile of village road, from each well-tended house or garden came a greeting, '*Eu-ora-na*', or a shyly given present, a band of shells for my pandanus hat, a necklace for Susan, or a drink of coconut milk; and if ever a dog barked at us, it was immediately stopped, as often as not by the children.

Although we wished to stay longer at this charming unspoilt place, and had received permission to do so, our future plans made it necessary for us to leave in mid-April. Once again the Gendarme piloted us through the reefs, and soon we passed out of that fair lagoon to the open sea, and regretfully leaving the Far Mountain astern, shaped a course for Tahiti, where mail should lie waiting for us, and where we could re-stock our nearly empty lockers.

6

Islomanes' Paradise

Our course lay through the southern part of the Tuamotu (sometimes known as the Dangerous Archipelago), a cluster of seventy-eight islands, nearly all of them atolls, which stand only a few feet above the sea; the atolls with palms growing on them are visible from a distance of between 5 and 7 miles. A glance at the *List of Lights* might give the impression that some trouble has been taken to make navigation through the Tuamotu a little less difficult, were it not for the remarks printed against each of the eight lights listed. These read: 'unreliable'; 'extinguished'; 'intended'; 'intended'; 'extinguished'; 'extinguished'; 'intended'; 'temporarily extinguished'. But we experienced no real difficulty, because the southern atolls are not so thickly clustered as are those in the central and northern parts of the archipelago, and it was possible to lay a course well clear of most of them.

However, we decided we would like to visit just one of the more remote atolls, and chose Mururoa, which lay very nearly on our course and 230 miles from Mangareva. The *Pacific Islands Pilot*, Vol. III, informed us that the lagoon, which is 15 miles long, is studded with coral heads and is mostly 20 fathoms deep, and that many islands, none of which is inhabited, stand on the reef. Like so many of the reefs and islands in the Pacific, everything about Mururoa is not precisely known. For example, the *Pilot* mentions that 'there are many more islets than are shown on the chart', and 'in 1948 the reef at its western end was reported to extend 5 miles farther westward than charted'. The place sounded interesting, and seemed to us to be well worth a visit, so we steered for it, but as we approached the weather degenerated, the sky clouded over, and a huge swell came rolling up from the direction of Cape Horn. Meanwhile the barometer, which for the past few days had made only the usual diurnal movements, was falling steadily. In these circumstances I did not care to anchor in that large lagoon where a shift of wind at night could place us in a dangerous situation; indeed, it would scarcely have been sensible to attempt to reach an anchorage, because reef pilotage by eye is impossible when the sky is overcast. Reluctantly we therefore passed the island by and stood on for Tahiti, but I have often since reproached myself for this, wondering where the line is properly drawn between seamanlike prudence in an ocean which has claimed many ships and faint-heartedness; the more so as our motto, carved in the companionway, reads 'Grab a chance and you won't be sorry for a might-have-been'.

Throughout the rest of the passage the weather was indifferent. After the overcast cleared it left the sky hazy, so that the stars shone only faintly and the sun was a woolly ball; often there were rain squalls of great intensity, each bringing a temporary change of wind, and always the great swell came rolling up from the Southern Sea, throwing the ship to leeward and causing the sails to slat noisily. Such conditions cause more wear and tear on the gear than does the longest gale.

On the eighth day at sea we sighted the remarkable cone of Mehetia rising stark into the evening sky ahead. We passed it at night, and at dawn, so clear was the atmosphere, we could see the 7,000-ft. mountains of Tahiti about 70 miles distant. But for the present that island was out of our reach; the wind fell lighter and lighter, the sails slammed more and more often, and by noon we were becalmed in great heat. We took the opportunity to clean the ship and ourselves, and Susan cut my hair, for after all it was Tahiti, 'pearl of the south seas', which lay ahead, and although we remembered Papeete, the port, as a dirty, down-at-heels little town, there would be other yachts and many visitors and we must look our best.

Ever since I took to doing this,' said Susan as she snipped

away with the rusty scissors, 'I have looked closely at other men's heads; they must often have wondered at my interest.'

At dusk, as we sat together in the cockpit enjoying our sundowner, the fabulous island, as though tired of being looked at, buried herself in an enormous black cloud, while overhead in ones and twos the stars came out. Not until the early hours of the morning did we start to move onwards again, when a faint air filled the light nylon ghoster. Soon the swell drew more aft, the sails went to sleep, and all through the forenoon we slipped silently and pleasantly along, enjoying the lovely sight of the bright green island which lay ahead, talking of it and discussing what we would do when we arrived. At noon with 25 miles still to go, it seemed unlikely that we would get in that day, but by then the sea had grown quite smooth in the lee of the land, and *Wanderer* slipped along with increased speed and little fuss, and so managed to arrive off Papeete Pass at sundown.

In shorts and shirt and pandanus hat with a string of shells around it, the Captain of the Port boarded us, for pilotage is compulsory there, and took us quietly and efficiently to a berth at the famous waterfront, where we dropped an anchor and took our sternlines to old cannon partly buried along the edge of the main road. He produced a few simple forms and helped us fill them in, while a crowd of Tahitians and yachtsmen gathered to inspect the new arrivals and ask their questions.

'Where are you from?'

'How many days out?'

'Seen anything of *Penella*? There's mail for her at the bank.'

For yachts Papeete is the crossroads of the Pacific, and there sooner or later you are sure to meet someone you know. So I was not surprised on looking up as a voice cried 'Hello, Eric!' to see Dr. Franklen-Evans, owner of the yawl *Kochab*, in which he had sailed from England to New Zealand a few years before, and was now on his way east towards the West Indies. Within the hour we were dining with him at the Diadem, a Chinese eating place. Afterwards we went on to Quinn's crowded bamboo hut, probably the most famous and uninhibited bar and night club in the southern hemisphere (even the w.c.s are

communal). With *heis* of cool, sweet-smelling flowers round our
necks, we drank Hinano (the local beer) and watched the lively
dancers on the close-packed floor—we even tried out our own
unsteady seagoing legs. It was all so familiar that we found it
difficult to believe that seven years had passed since our last
visit; and that night, as we turned into our bunks, our ears were
filled with the familiar sounds of Tahiti: gusts of high-pitched
laughter, the stutter of auto-cycles and generating plants, the
thrum of a guitar, and voices singing. The scents, too, were
strongly familiar: French tobacco, *tiare Tahiti* (sweet and
heady), and petrol fumes.

Along the waterfront there was a considerable gathering of
yachts, including *Si Ye Pambili*, which we had met at Barbados,
with our friends Bill Baker and Roger Gowen aboard, and most
evenings one or other of the yachts gave a rum-punch party.
Usually the parties were enlivened by the presence of some of
the girls from Quinn's, who are in the habit of adopting yachts,
particularly those with pleasant young bachelor crews, such as
Pambili, and usually live aboard; they take over the washing
and cooking, and fill every other available moment with guitar
playing and song. The songs are either gay or sad, for there are
no half measures with the Tahitians, and all have wonderful
rhythm. But there was one rude little song, if one can call it
that, for it was more a form of greeting than a song, which was
all the rage during our visit. The first time we heard it was one
evening at Quinn's, where one of the girls who was about to
perform the erotic *tamure* up on the tiny balcony above the
dance floor parted the bamboo screen, leant her slender, grass-
skirted and flower-bedecked body dangerously far over the
edge, and addressing herself to me sang:

> 'Hello, capitaine, how are you?
> Hello, capitaine, how are you?
> I lofe you,
> Yes, I do;
> God-damn son-of-a-bitch,
> What's the matter, you?'

She accompanied her song with gestures and grimaces, and

ended with a bewitching smile which included Susan as well as me. In any other place we would have felt embarrassed; but this was Papeete, and the song and the roar of laughter which followed it seemed quite natural there.

Soon after her arrival *Pambili* was adopted by a particularly charming girl, Noéline, and a friend of hers. Susan and I spent several evenings aboard, and the girls readily accepted us and treated us with tact and friendliness. They co-operated willingly when we made tape-recordings of their songs, addressed us in the Tahitian manner as *mama* and *papa*, and kissed us whenever they thought it was necessary, so passing on the virulent cold which at that time was ravaging the waterfront. When we left late at night the girls always came to the rail to sing haunting, melancholy *Bon Voyage* as we rowed back to *Wanderer*.

After we had got to know her a little I asked Noéline to perform the *tamure* one afternoon so that we might make a movie sequence of that exciting dance, consisting mainly of fast undulations of the hips, which send shimmering ripples down the long, well-combed grass skirt. Although this should be danced beneath the palms in the moonlight to the scalp-tickling beat of drums, and not on the deck of a yacht in the heat of the day to the music from a gramophone, she readily agreed, rehearsed painstakingly, allowed me to garland her with flowers, and performed enchantingly. After the filming was over I gave her a little packet containing a green brooch which Susan and I had got for her. She took it down into the cabin, but a few moments later returned in tears, pushed the brooch into my pocket, and said:

'I cannot take this, for it would remind me of you and *mama* when you have gone, and I would be too sad.'

Noéline has three children, all with white blood in them, of which she is very proud.

There is a certain magic in the word Tahiti, and for those whom the Americans call islomanes it is the supreme symbol

PLATE 13
We still regard Moorea as the most beautiful island in the world. *Wanderer* sails up Paopao Bay to reach an anchorage near its head 2 miles from the sea.

of escape. Together with neighbouring Moorea—said to be James Michener's Bali Ha'i of *South Pacific*—it comprises the classical setting of the unspoiled Polynesian dream of leaning palms, dazzling beaches (most in reality are of black sand), and translucent water. The people are warm, easygoing, and not much bothered by the failures of yesterday or the worries of the future; but although the women are shapely, they are not all beautiful—a measure of Chinese blood is needed for that—and, despite the travel brochures, most wear conventional clothing; indeed, the French insist on this in the town. Naturally the fact that Tahiti, far out in the central South Pacific, was not easy of access, was one of its chief attractions. But shortly after our visit something happened which may well prove to be the most important interruption in the island's history since Cook landed there in 1769—the completion of a runway capable of accommodating large jet aircraft. The fortnightly flying-boat service from New Zealand has been abandoned, and planes now fly in direct from the States, bringing their loads of camera-festooned and dollar-laden tourists. The net result can scarcely be to the island's benefit in the long run, although the French, who have controlled the island for 120 years, have reluctantly decided that it needs an economic shot in the arm, and that seemed to be the only way of administering it. Hitherto the Tahitians have not been much interested in money. Their island provided most of their needs, and they worked for others only if they liked them or got fun out of the work itself. But with the tourist invasion money will flow more easily and bring with it the desire for more money, so the dancing, the feasting, and the singing may lose their friendly, improvised quality and become mere attractions on a package-tour agenda.

Wishing to see something more of Tahiti than just the harbour and the town, we sailed away one day through the lagoon inside the barrier reef, and, doing the pilotage by eye from up

PLATE 14
Top: In Robinson Cove we lay near Tiger Tooth Mountain in perfect shelter, and (*bottom*) took a line to a palm and hauled the stern so close in to the steep beach that we could step off the bumkin into knee-deep water and wade ashore.

aloft—that is the best procedure in coral waters, and provided the sun is high and not ahead, one can judge the depth by the colour—found a pleasant anchorage at Taapuna. There we lay in glass-clear water close to the reef, and spent many hours in the dinghy, drifting over its colourful mysteries and photographing them; to make this possible without an under-water camera or a glass-bottomed box, we used an umbrella to kill the reflections on the surface.

During the evening of 22 May, while we were still at Taapuna, we heard on the radio a report of severe earthquakes in Chile, accompanied by great loss of life. Susan and I decided that these might cause tidal or seismic seawaves, but we did not take the matter very seriously with Chile some 4,000 miles away, for we did not then know that such waves can travel immense distances at 490 miles per hour. The waves started to reach us during the night, but the lagoon being well protected by the reef, they reached a height inside of only 5 ft. Apart from inundating some blocks of buildings at Papeete, they did little harm and they caused us no inconvenience. For the following twenty-four hours a diminishing wave pulse silently and mysteriously covered and uncovered the reefs at intervals of between five and ten minutes.

Naturally the best place to be during the onset of seismic waves is out in the open ocean, where, well away from the land, the waves may be no more than 1 or 2 ft. high with a length of 20 miles, so in spite of their great speed they will, of course, pass unnoticed. It is not until they reach shallow water or land that they slow down, increase in height, and become dangerous, particularly to vessels lying in shallow or unprotected anchorages. The waves of 22 and 23 May caused damage as far from their source as New Zealand, Australia, New Caledonia, and Japan.

During our two circumnavigations we have visited many islands in the three great oceans, and we still regard Moorea, Tahiti's near neighbour, as the most beautiful of all. Measuring only 9 miles by 7, it rises above the narrow coastal strip in fantastic jagged peaks and spires to a height of nearly 4,000 ft.

Several of the spires are pierced like the eyes of needles. The island is encircled by a barrier reef, through which there are several wide and easy passes; two on its sheltered northern shore give access to two deep bays—except for the palms and the weather, they might well be fjords in Norway—which thrust in among the mountains for a distance of 2 miles. It was into the most easterly of these, Paopao Bay, that we sailed at the end of the month; we entered in a rain squall, which temporarily hid the mountains and bridged the pass with its vivid rainbow, and anchored near several of the yachts which we had already met at Papeete—two American, one Canadian, and two up from New Zealand. *Penella* came in soon after, and that was the last time on this voyage that we were to see Leigh and Dorrie, of whom we had grown fond, for we had shared several anchorages with that enthusiastic couple. Already, though not yet at the half-way point of the present voyage, they were talking about their second circumnavigation and hinting at a third. At Moorea our tracks separated. *Penella* went west by a different route and reached Brisbane, and three years later we had news of her still there, but with plans on the boil for a move very soon.

The nightly parties, which had been such a feature of our stay at Papeete, naturally continued at Moorea, and sometimes we all rowed up to the head of the bay after supper to visit what the New Zealanders in their descriptive way called 'the top boozer'. There the landlord played the accordion and sang Tahitian songs, the words coming, apparently, not from his mouth but from some sonorous cavern in the region of his heart, ventriloquous fashion. The red wine circulated freely, and we danced and danced again on the sand-sprinkled floor in the harsh, green light from a pressure lamp, while in through the wide-open windows drifted the sweetshop scent of drying vanilla. The moon seemed strangely large and bright and rather disapproving as we made our zigzag courses back to the anchorage in our assorted dinghies.

It was at Moorea that we became friendly with Stuart and Emily Riddell, owners of the ketch *Romayne*, homeward bound for Canada at the end of a long Pacific cruise. We had first met at a party aboard *Pambili*, where Emily, a handsome and vivacious girl from the U.S.A., with long, graceful legs which, I am sure, would be the envy of any ballet dancer, insisted on trying to teach me the *hula*. As one of the New Zealand 'yachties' remarked:

'It's odd to watch an American girl married to a Canadian teaching an Englishman to dance the *hula* aboard a Rhodesian yacht in a French Polynesian port, before an audience including Chileans, Australians, New Zealanders, and Frenchmen.'

I feared at the time that Emily was up to no good.

'Lift your knees higher. Now squat down on the deck and reach out towards me. Oh! come on, and act as though you are interested.'

But at Moorea Emily and her husband came aboard at our invitation one morning, and they did us the honour of staying without even glancing at their watches until sundown, and the party only broke up then because we all had an engagement aboard another yacht. In my slow way I began to realize that Emily had tried to teach me to *hula* simply out of kindness, because she honestly felt that I was not getting all I should out of the evening.

Two miles to the west along Moorea's northern coast lies Papetoai Bay, which if possible is even more beautiful than Paopao, but is not so often visited. We made our way into its silent depths, over which the ramparts of Tiger Tooth Mountain cast their shadows, and came to an anchorage in Robinson Cove. The shore there is free of fringing reef, and it shoals so steeply that after we had dropped our anchor in 9 fathoms of dark green water, we were able to take a line to a palm tree and haul *Wanderer*'s stern so close in to the beach that, although her rudder was in 7 ft., it was possible to walk out along the bumkin and step into knee-deep water. That was how we went ashore to collect the crisp French loaf which the Chinese baker left each day in the cockroach-infested box beside the road.

Robinson Cove is one of the most perfect anchorages we know. Overlapping points of land shut out the pass and the wider part of the bay; the narrow beach is of clean, coarse, yellow sand, and is shaded by the palms; people in the occasional vehicle using the road, which there is little more than a track with grass growing between the wheel-ruts, always waved and shouted '*Bonjour*' or '*Eu-ora-na*' as they passed. At that point the coastal plain is only 400 yds. wide, and is planted with coconut palms, their serried ranks fading away into cool green distances like the pillars of a dimly lit church. The plain stops abruptly at the foot of a cliff which rises almost sheer for over 2,000 ft. The top of the cliff is usually shrouded in mist, and by night the cold air comes sliding down to make the cove so pleasantly cool and damp that sometimes we needed blankets on our bunks, and that in a small yacht in the tropics, where one is usually overheated, is the height of luxury. The faint rustle of palm fronds in the breeze, the splash of a jumping fish, and the occasional crash as a nut tumbled to the ground—these were the only sounds to disturb the stillness of the nights.

Our second visit to Tahiti had been more enjoyable than our earlier one, probably because we arrived there later and therefore met more yachts; the crews of all of them spoke our own language and we soon became friendly with them. The lights and noise and bustle of the waterfront, the singing, the dancing, and the parties, had provided a not unpleasant change after the vast wastes of the empty ocean and the unsophisticated islands at which we had touched; but now we were both glad to get away from the artificialities of the town and to live in absolute peace for a few days before tearing ourselves away from this islomanes' paradise and heading for Rarotonga, most important of the Cook Islands, 600 miles away to the west-south-west, where we knew we could expect to find no idyllic anchorages such as this.

7

Towards Fiji

The trade wind seemed to be almost as reluctant to carry us away from French Oceania as we were to leave, and it fell so light that on one day we achieved a run of only 7 miles, which was the poorest *Wanderer* had ever done. However, we knew from our own experiences and those of other voyagers that almost anything that will float is capable of blowing down wind as far as Tahiti, but west of that island one can no longer rely on a steady, fair wind, and other difficulties arise.

However, the passage to the Cook Islands was uneventful except for two things: we fell in with an enormous school of porpoises, and we made a bad landfall. It was during breakfast that we heard the porpoises coming. They made a tremendous commotion as they approached from the north-east, splashing, blowing, and whistling, and soon we were surrounded. The sea all round and beneath us was so thick with swift-moving, interlacing, graceful bodies, that it would scarcely have been possible to dive in among them without collision; the surface was crowded with others who with backs and fins projecting seemed to be basking. We estimated their number to exceed three hundred. They remained with us for an hour, and then, just as though an order had been given, the whole lot suddenly got under way and quickly vanished in a westerly direction.

As we approached the Cooks, the wind headed us off our course, and we found it desirable to pass between the outlying islands of Mitiaro and Mauke, instead of passing south of both, as we had originally intended. At dawn of our seventh day at sea, when Mauke should have lain 25 miles ahead, we were astonished to sight it about 10 miles away just abaft the beam. This really did shake the navigation department, and for a while I wondered if I had lost the day of the week, and had been using the wrong date when consulting the *Nautical Almanac* while working out my observations. But a morning sight confirmed the longitude exactly, and as I now had no reason to doubt the accuracy of the previous day's sights, which had been taken in ideal conditions, it was obvious that we had come within the influence of a strong, favourable current; nevertheless, something more than 25 miles of current in 20 hours is a lot, considering that there had been no noticeable current throughout the previous six days.

Three months after this incident the New Zealand yacht *Margaret*, while on passage from Bora-Bora towards Rarotonga, ran ashore during a very dark night on Mitiaro's fringing reef. The watch-keeper had seen the faint grey line of breakers ahead, but as the mainsail was not set at the time the yacht was unable to claw off. She started to break up at once, and her crew of three waded ashore through the surf, their feet being badly cut by the sharp coral, and were well looked after by the kindly natives until the yacht *Patsy Jean* picked them up. Something of a mystery has been made of the loss of *Margaret*, but in view of our own experience in that neighbourhood, it seems reasonable to suppose that the unsuspected current was responsible. Possibly current can also be blamed for the loss of the fine ship *Runic* a few months later on Middleton Reef; no doubt she had every available navigational aid, but navigation is not yet an exact science.

Rarotonga has no barrier reef to give its anchorages shelter, but on its north coast, and about half a mile apart, there are two small breaks in the fringing reef comprising the harbours of Avarua and Avatiu. Their entrances are only 70 ft. wide, and the harbours themselves are little more than that in width and are apt to be congested with schooners and lighters, for most of the produce and requirements of the group are brought there for trans-shipment. We arrived in the evening just half an hour too late to see the way in; so we spent the night jilling about in the offing, and headed in for Avatiu after breakfast. We could see that a number of vessels lay within, and the entrance, with the swell breaking on both sides, looked very narrow. As we approached, two dinghies came out and stationed themselves one at each side of the entrance. We found they were manned by two New Zealand cruising men, Don Silk and Bob Boyd, owner and crew of *Patsy Jean*, who had come out to guard the reefs and show us the way in. We slipped in between them, squeezed past the schooner *Tiare Taporo*, which like a spider in its web lay in the middle of the harbour moored all fours to anchors set on the reefs, and rounded up astern of her as directed by our helpers, who took our lines and made them fast, for there is no room for anchoring. A little breathless, we were then able to thank our helpers and look about us. It certainly was an odd little spot we had come to, not much more than a crack in the reef. The wind, then blowing fresh from the north, whistled in the rigging, and the roar of breakers and the damp feel of spume enveloped us. Ahead of us the schooner pitched sedately, for the onshore wind was sending a slight swell into the harbour. She was an old-timer skippered by the famous Andy Thomson, almost a legendary figure, then in his eightieth year. Owned by the big Pacific trading firm A. B. Donald, her job was to carry passengers and goods among the scattered islands of the group, none of which have harbours, so trans-shipment has to be done in her own open, double-ended boats through the breakers. Astern of us five yachts lay in a narrow gut between tumbledown jetties, and a sixth was hauled out on the shore. With two trading vessels in the other harbour, and the Government ship *Maui Pomare* anchored outside, it was the largest gathering of vessels Rarotonga had ever known.

That evening ashore we chanced upon Hughie Williams.

PLATE 15
Top: Avatiu Harbour, Rarotonga, is little more than a crack in the fringing reef, and it was here that the tidal waves following the Chilean earthquake caused such damage. On the left lies the old trading schooner *Tiare Taporo*. *Bottom:* Vava'u was loud with the noise of mallets hammering out the bark of the *hiapo* tree to make *tapa*-cloth, a material which is used for bedding, curtains, and clothes.

We had met him seven years before at Tahiti shortly after he had sailed the Brixham trawler *Inspire* out from England. He pushed us into his shining new station wagon along with his *vahine*, an attractive Cook Island girl, and within a few moments we reached Avarua Harbour and went aboard the trader *Dobri*, which he now owned and skippered. He gave us 'tea' of steak and chips, while cockroaches made their furtive way beneath the edges of the tablecloth, and told us of his many adventures and the money he had made as an independent ship-owning trader—a remarkable story of courage and resource.

'I've had as many ships as I've had women,' he ended proudly and, apparently, without a thought for his *vahine* sitting there between us, 'each one bigger and better than the last, and I've wrecked none of 'em.'

During the night of the tidal waves, when we were safely in the lagoon at Tahiti, there were three yachts lying in Avatiu. The harbour is shallow, and after each 12 ft. wave (they came at intervals of seven or eight minutes) it dried right out so that the yachts lay over on their bilges, with masts and rigging entangled, only to be picked up and flung against one another and the coral shore as the next wave surged in with a roar across the reefs. Two of the yachts were severely damaged, one so badly that she filled, and both of them lost their masts. The third received only superficial damage. This disaster did not dismay the practical and resourceful New Zealanders. With help and materials borrowed from the Public Works Department they built themselves a slip; in turn they hauled each yacht out and repaired her, and by the time we arrived all were practically ready for sea once more.

The Cook Islands are administered by New Zealand, and several of the New Zealand families living on Rarotonga, including the Resident Commissioner and Mrs. Nevill, invited us

PLATE 16
Top: Uninhabited Yaukuve, a tiny island within the Great Astrolabe Reef, where the only footprints on the beach were our own. *Bottom:* Only by using a tripod and a delayed-action release was it possible for both of us to appear together in a still or movie picture.

to their homes for meals and showed us most of the island and its way of life. After such kindness it may seem in poor taste to mention that we gained the impression (and it was nothing more) that Rarotonga is over-administered, and that perhaps rather too much is being done at considerable cost for the unappreciative islanders, many of whom wish to leave it for New Zealand the moment there is an opportunity, and the chance occurs more often now that cruise ships call offering £50 passages. The export of oranges and tomatoes was being encouraged, and the small, haphazard packing stations had been closed in favour of a big modern one near the port, which de-buttons, washes, dries, grades, and packs the fruit, with the result that the New Zealand tax-payer pays a good deal more than he imagines for his Cook Island oranges.

We had always found Polynesians to be honest folk, so were surprised to discover that the Rarotongans will steal almost anything, not even drawing the line at their neighbours' chickens. Visiting yachts are not exempt. One, which had been damaged by the tidal waves, had many things stolen from her while she lay helplessly on the shore, and someone cut the inshore end off our nylon warp—presumably to make fishing lines, for fishing is a whole-time business with the jetty loafers— so leaving *Wanderer* in a dangerous situation in our absence. However, like all Polynesians, these people are friendly and kind, and we could not help but like them and their pleasant island.

We were not entirely sorry to leave our uneasy and restricted berth, which we thought could become a dangerous trap in certain conditions, although it is true that *Tiare Taporo* once rode out a cyclone there with thirty-seven lines holding her to the reefs on either hand.

Bound for Fiji by way of the Tonga Islands, we found the south-east trade blowing fresh when we left, and by evening, when we were 25 miles out from the lee of the island, it had risen to near gale force. So we hove-to under the close-reefed mainsail only, expecting the wind to moderate by dawn; but it did not, and the following evening was blowing a lot harder,

and the sea became so rough that we started to ship heavy water
forward. We therefore took the sail in, and that was not so
difficult as it may sound, because the sail was already much
reduced in area by the deep reef, and there is a permanent
boom gallows extending nearly the full beam of the ship. I
watched to see how she would behave lying a-hull beam on to
wind and sea, and Susan went below. The ship seemed to be
doing well enough for the present, and after a few minutes I
turned to slide open the hatch and follow Susan, when a violent
lurch flung me to leeward. I was brought up sharply with the
lee sheet winch in my chest, and broke a rib. Thereafter I was
of little use and had to leave everything to Susan for some days.
She bound me up, but I did not recover as quickly as I might
have done, because I could get no proper rest in my wildly
heaving bunk. The following afternoon the weather had wor-
sened; the wind had increased to 45 knots according to our
anemometer, that is force 9, a strong gale. The ship was no
longer happy, and from time to time she shipped heavy water
over the weather side; the weathercloth lashed to the guardrail to windward of the cockpit was carried away, and one of
the stanchion sockets was uprooted and bent over at 45 deg.
Clearly it was no longer advisable to lie a-hull; but we did not
wish to turn and run before the wind either with or without
draglines towing astern, for that would have called for a helmsman and I did not feel equal to standing a watch; also, dead
down wind lay a vigia, 'breakers reported 1945', which we
must avoid at all costs. So we streamed the sea-anchor—this
was from a Catalina flying boat and has an oval mouth measuring 3 ft. by 2 ft.—over the stern on a 30-fathom nylon line. The
ship then lay with wind and sea a little out on the quarter, her
drift was barely one knot, and she seemed happy once more; so
we left her like that to look after herself for the next 2 days and
16 hours, except that Susan frequently struggled into oilskins
and went out into the driving spray to renew the chafing gear
where the warp passed through the fairlead and round the
samson post. Throughout that time we both felt sick, and
could manage to eat only an occasional scrambled egg, or a

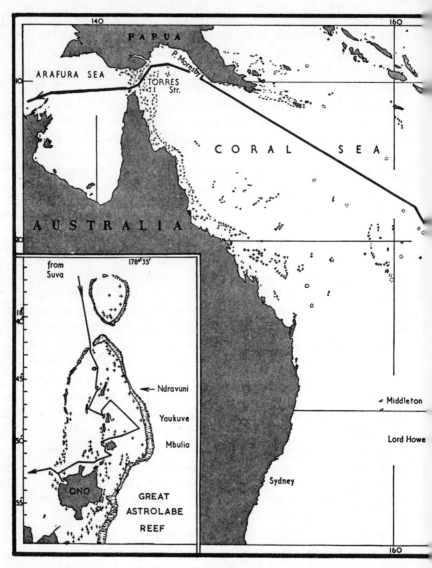

WESTERN PART OF SOUTH PACIFIC WITH IN

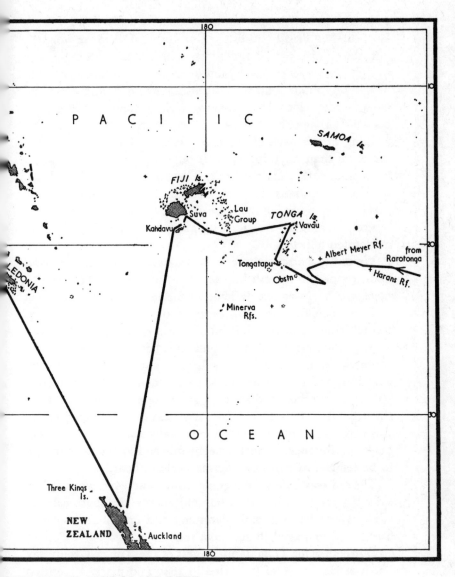

THE GREAT ASTROLABE REEF

little of the excellent currant loaf the kind Nevills had given us. We dozed and read and listened to the wind. And we worried, not about any specific thing, for *Wanderer* had been through this kind of weather several times before, and surely any weakness in her hull or gear would have shown up before now; and we were moving so slowly that the vigia to leeward had not yet become an anxiety. Yet worry was there, a nameless little nagging at the back of the mind, caused, I believe, more by the noise than anything else. 'If only it would stop . . . just for a moment!' But it doesn't. There comes a time when in spite of it all, and exhausted, perhaps, by the mental fret, one gets to sleep in spite of the noise and the motion, and on waking several hours later, realizes with great relief that the wind has moderated a little.

We did not attempt to get the sea-anchor in until the wind had dropped to a fresh breeze; then, with the warp round a sheet winch, it was not difficult for Susan to rattle in a few feet of slack each time the ship dropped down the back of a sea. But to bring the sea-anchor inboard was quite another matter, for we do not rig it with a tripping line, because that is liable to cause chafe. In an attempt to help, I climbed over the after guardrail and out on to the bumkin, but there I was in such pain from my damaged rib that, sweating and trembling, I lay there helpless for a little while, capable only of clinging on. It was with some difficulty that I eventually managed to clamber back into the cockpit. Susan meanwhile had somehow managed in her efficient way to get the sea-anchor aboard.

The sea was a long time going down, and even when it had subsided we were left with our old enemy the south-easterly swell, which had our sails slamming and crashing as soon as Susan had managed to get them set.

Our course for Tongatapu, largest of the Tonga Group, lay north of Harans Reef (reported in 1842 and marked 'position doubtful') and south of Albert Meyer Reef (reported in 1911); we steered to give both as wide a berth as possible, for, as is always the way with vigias, it was probable that neither lay in its charted position. Our eleventh day at sea, when we were by

account 25 miles from Albert Meyer Reef, was overcast, and
the wind was again freshening from the south-east. We ran fast
on our way with the boom occasionally plunging its end
shudderingly into the rising sea. By midnight, with the wind
up to near gale force, and when we were only about 120 miles
from an anchorage at Tongatapu, we did not care to continue
running towards a reef-fringed lee shore with so much wind, for
the overcast had prevented sights being taken, and we were not
certain of our position. So once more we hove-to.

Considering that this was not the cyclone season and that
we were still within the supposed south-east trade-wind belt,
the wind behaved strangely, working round anti-clockwise
through every point of the compass in turn. At its height in the
early hours of 30 July I logged it as a strong gale, and later,
when we reached Tongatapu, we had confirmation of its
strength—a church and some houses had been blown down, the
new Tongan ocean-going tug *Hifofua* had dragged her anchor
and gone aground on a reef, and a Japanese tuna-fishing vessel
had been lost, it was reported, with all hands. Two years later
Tuaikepau, a small Tongan vessel, with seventeen men aboard,
stranded on one of the Minerva Reefs, which lie about 260 miles
south-west of Tongatapu, and began to break up next day. The
survivors made their way across to the wreck of a Japanese
fishing vessel on the same reef, and which was believed to be
the same that was lost at the time *Wanderer* was in the neighbourhood. They had only enough food and water for ten days;
after that they lived for more than three months on fish and
shellfish and distilled water, presumably using wood from the
wreck as fuel. From this same wreck they built a raft on which
two men drifted north-west for 350 miles to a Fijian island to
raise the alarm, with the result that most of the remaining
people were rescued.

Because of the constantly shifting wind, the sea where we
were never reached any great height, though it was much confused, and *Wanderer* did not ship any dangerously heavy water.
But the gale was too much for the tiny scrap of sail we had set
and that vibrated furiously; but I did not feel strong enough to

venture on deck to take it in, and I could not let Susan go, willing though she was. However, that tough piece of terylene survived undamaged. The high-pitched moan of the wind, and the shuddering of the ship as the sail shook her, were unnerving, and as our original position was uncertain and it was not possible to keep an accurate reckoning because of the shifting wind, we were much worried by Gleaner Reef and a reported 'obstruction', which dangers in turn lay to leeward of us. I do not know what the word 'obstruction' means when printed on a chart with depths of 3,000 and 4,000 fathoms close each side of it. It cannot mean a minefield, unlit buoy, or similar man-made booby-trap such as one sometimes finds in or near a naval base; yet if a shoal, reef, breakers, or discoloured water had been reported, it seems reasonable to suppose that the chart or *Pilot* would say so.

During that second gale we drifted 80 miles away from Tongatapu. As soon as it moderated sufficiently, and after we had obtained some observations of the sun with which to fix our position, we let draw and hurried back towards the island. On the way we crossed the Tonga Trench, which with a sounding of 5,375 fathoms, i.e. about 6 miles, is a very deep part of the ocean (Everest is about 5 miles high). The greatest known ocean depth is 6,033 fathoms in the Mariana Trench, and the recent report that H.M. Surveying Ship *Cook* had found a depth of 6,297 fathoms in a narrow trench east of the Philippines has proved to be incorrect.

During the forenoon of our sixteenth day at sea we occasionally sighted Eua, southernmost of the Tonga Group, as we were lifted up on the swell. Although the wind was still strong, we made more sail, for there was just a chance that we might get in that evening before dark. We heartened ourselves with a bottle of wine with our lunch as we drove on, bow wave sparkling, hissing wake streaming out and over the high following sea, rich brown mainsail slashing crazy arcs across the sky. We tore in between Eua and Eua Iki, where, miraculously, the high sea subsided without confusion, and in wonderfully smooth water beneath a cloudless sky swept in through the

eastern approach channel, where to starboard lay a chain of
little windswept motus, with palms so tightly packed that there
was no room for more, and the outermost leant seaward on all
sides. We wriggled through the narrows, and still with plenty
of light to see the reefs, made our way across the large and
poorly sheltered bay towards the town of Nuku'alofa, the capital
of Tonga. There, sheltered by a row of graceful but strangely
out-of-place Norfolk pines, stood Queen Salote's little timber-
built Alice-in-Wonderland palace.

We had been told that there is a boat harbour at Nuku'alofa,
although no mention of it is made in the Admiralty publications,
and sure enough, as we approached the fringing reef east of
the town, we saw a thicket of masts close inshore. Hurriedly
we handed the sails and started the motor, for this appeared to
be no place for the stranger to go blundering into, and cautiously we nosed our way along the channel cut through the reef
to the snug but very crowded little basin. Somehow we managed
to turn round, and with the willing help of crews from off the
small cutters and launches which inhabited the place, inserted
ourselves into the only vacant berth.

How very glad we were to be motionless at last and out of
reach of the tearing wind. We had taken 16 days to make good
a distance of 858 miles, and of that time we had spent 3 days
14 hours hove-to, 1 day 9 hours lying a-hull, and 2 days 16 hours
lying to the sea-anchor. Some trip!

Tonga consists of more than a hundred islands, extending
from Eua at the south end of the group to Vava'u, nearly 200
miles to the nor'-nor'-east. Most of them are low and lie in a
bewildering maze of coral reefs, but the group is bordered at
its western edge by a chain of volcanic islands, some of them
active, which rise high above the sea and make good landmarks.
The only kingdom in the southern hemisphere, Tonga is ruled
by big, genial, efficient Queen Salote Tupou, whose eldest son,
Crown Prince Tungi, is Premier; with its exports of bananas
and copra, it is remarkable in balancing its budget. The people
are Polynesian, and are said to surpass all other Pacific islanders
in mental development, but after the gay and carefree Society

Islanders we found them rather ponderous and sober. They are a highly religious people, and most of their actions are dictated by the Church; there are many denominations, and probably more churches to the square mile than in any other place that we have visited. Cook gave the name Friendly Islands to the group.

For eight days *Wanderer* lay in the Fa'ua boat harbour at Nuku'alofa, with an anchor out ahead, lines to her neighbours, and chains to the shore. We used chains because the bollards were set back a long way from the water, and chafe caused by the wheels of passing traffic was considerable. Tired though we were, our sleep was disturbed, for, as is usual in most commercial ports, there were people who went to bed late, and others who got up early; in addition, there were some who stayed up all night, coughing, talking, and spitting within a few feet of us. Also there was much coming and going of inter-island boats, packed with passengers (Pacific islanders will always travel if there is anything to travel in), and there were tremendous scenes of welcome and farewell. *Wanderer* was a bit in their way, but nobody seemed to mind that, and the boats were well handled. But unfortunately the Eua ferry, when wriggling into a restricted berth just ahead of us, got a turn of our chain round her propeller and damaged four links in the middle of a 30-fathom length.

We experienced much kindness, never a day passing without an invitation to a meal or a drive, or offers of assistance with any small jobs we had in hand. The British Agent and Consul, and Mrs. Coode, invited us to a cocktail party at the consulate, where I met Crown Prince Tungi and his brother, Prince Tu'ipelehake. The former is much interested in shipping, and partly for that reason, Tonga was able to claim, for her size of population (60,000), to own the largest merchant fleet in the world. She possessed a cargo ship, an oil barge, two inter-island vessels, and an oceangoing tug. Unfortunately the new tuna-fishing vessel, built in Japan, was mysteriously lost with all hands on her maiden trip.

As in the Azores, whales are harpooned and killed from open

sailing boats, and there were four kills during our stay. After each kill as many boats as were in the neighbourhood, usually five or six, made fast their lines and with sails full and drawing, and with huge black flags flying from their mastheads to signify a kill, towed the submerged carcass slowly in and beached it at high water on the edge of the fringing reef. As soon as the tide had fallen sufficiently, the business of flenching began, and the islanders in their hundreds came from all parts on foot, by horse, bicycle, or truck (which here serves as bus), and waded out across the shallows to buy their four shillings-worth of fat red meat. After twenty-four hours the remains were towed out into the bay to be eaten by sharks, and for a few days shark fishing was the chief occupation. With their love of fat meat, especially pig (in the market you can buy meat for next to nothing if you let them cut the fat off to sell to someone else), it is perhaps not surprising that the Tongan is stout, and this is emphasized by the *ta'ovala*, a woven mat worn tied or belted round the waist. The Queen likes the *ta'ovala* to be worn— there are different sorts for various occasions, the *ta'ovala* worn at funerals, for example, is of coarse texture and covers the body from chest to ankles—and no Tongan may enter the palace grounds without one.

There is no public water supply on Tongatapu; rain caught on roofs and stored in tanks is the chief source. But there had not been much rain lately, so before we left we got our supply from the smart red fire-engine, and paid 11s. for 600 gallons. We never discovered where it came from or who had the remaining 530 gallons.

There are four channels of approach through the reefs to Nuku'alofa. We had come in through the eastern one and we left by the north-western channel, which is marked by buoys and leading beacons. Our intention was to visit Vava'u, an island which we had tried to visit seven years before after leaving Samoa, and had got to within 8 miles of its harbour only to be blown away by a great gale. We chose a course which lay to the west of the low islands and reefs comprising the centre of Tonga, and between them and the chain of volcanoes to which I have already referred. The south-east trade would be on the beam, and with reefs and islands close to windward, we looked forward to a fast and pleasant trip in smooth water. But it did not turn out like that; by the time we had reached open water the wind had hauled round to north of east, so that we could not always lay the course, and with no shelter to windward the motion was abominable and progress slow.

We sailed to windward of the site of Falcon Island, an island which from time to time mysteriously appears and disappears. In 1936, for example, it was 1 mile long and 200 ft. high, yet today the site of it is said to have a depth of 9 fathoms over it. During our first night out we passed the high islands of Tofua (still active) and Kao; the latter is a magnificent cone rising to a height of 3,000 ft., and even in the dark was impressive. All next day we could see ahead the cone of yet another volcano, Late Island, but our progress to windward was so slow that by nightfall we had not yet sighted Vava'u. We beat on for a while, looking for the 12-mile light which the chart and the *List of Lights* showed at the seaward end of the approach to Vava'u Harbour, for we felt that with its help we might be able to work into more sheltered water. But seeing nothing of it we hove-to and waited for daylight, and it was just as well that we did so, for when we passed close to the small island on which the light is said to stand, we saw no sign of the light or of any erection that could have housed it.

The approach to the harbour leads through an archipelago of large and small islands, some with sand beaches, others with cliffs so undercut by the sea that there is no access to them. So deep is the water among them, and so steeply do the islands or their fringing reefs rise, that although we spent a whole day sailing among them, we failed to find an anchorage at which to remain for the night. However, we did find Swallows' Cave, which is featured on the 3d. Tongan postage stamp, and in turns rowed in to its dark, echoing recesses, where the ink-black water sucked dolefully at the sheer rock walls, and watched *Wanderer*, framed in the opening, sailing in the sunlight outside.

The harbour at Vava'u is landlocked and spacious, but like the surrounding waters is much too deep. Mostly the soundings are between 20 and 30 fathoms, and although there is a shelf near the quay with only a couple of fathoms over it, the space is so restricted with coral patches that we, knowing the monthly steamer from New Zealand had called recently, secured to her hauling-off buoy, an enormous thing against which we bumped at times when there was insufficient wind to hold us off.

Vava'u was loud with the noise of mallets hammering out the bark of the *hiapo* tree to make *tapa*-cloth, a material which is used for bedding, curtains and clothing, and with the singing of hymns. There were only four white people on the island, and we invited them off to tea; in return the headmistress of the Free Wesleyan Mission girls' school asked us to go one evening to listen to her girls singing. We entered the school hall through a door leading straight on to the *tapa*-covered dais, and there before us, dressed in white and sitting cross-legged on the mat-covered floor, were 260 Tongan girls ranging in age from 12 to 20 years. They rose as we entered, their earnest faces shining in the harsh light from pressure lamps hanging over-head, and without accompaniment sang beautifully a number of hymns and the Lord's Prayer, a Tongan teacher conducting with clutching, drawing motions of her hands. We were deeply impressed, and when the headmistress asked if we had had enough, I replied that we would like to hear just one genuine Tongan song.

'Mr. Hiscock, do you not know what the day of the week is?' She looked shocked.

'Why, yes,' I said, 'it's Sunday.'

'Well, in Tonga no work and no play is permitted on the Sabbath.'

We left Vava'u at the end of August, bound for Suva, capital of Fiji, 460 miles away, and laid a course to pass through the wide passage at the southern end of the Lau, or Eastern, Group of Fiji, as being the most straightforward, though not quite the most direct, route. After an indifferent spell with a lot of rain, the weather appeared to be settled, and the wind was back in its proper quarter, south-east, but light. At midnight we were becalmed in the lee of Late Island. By the light of the moon I got a vertical sextant angle of its summit which placed us 4 miles away, yet we could clearly see the flash of high-driven spray and hear the roar of surf.

The fine weather continued through part of the second day, but at dusk a bank of heavy black cloud was moving up from the south-west, our courses converging, and soon the wind began to pipe up, calling for a reduction of sail. At midnight we were south of the Lau Group, and there altered course to pass between the high islands of Totoya and Matuku, 90 miles ahead. Then heavy rain set in, and apart from an occasional violent squall, killed the wind. We sheeted the boom amidships and tried to get some sleep, but the sea was confused and the squalls disquieting.

At about that time a saltwater boil on Susan's hand became inflamed and painful, and she came out in a rash. On three previous occasions she had suffered from serious blood poisoning, and as we now feared a fourth attack she started taking M. and B.

Throughout the next day the rain continued and was heavy at times. We sailed on, but no sights were possible, and as we did not wish to approach the islands, which are encircled by reefs, by night in such poor visibility from a position of which we were not sure, we hove-to at nightfall. The sea was still confused, but was growing larger, and the wind was near gale force at times. Our squeamish supper consisted of a cup of soup each. The whole of Susan's arm had swollen, her temperature was high, she felt far from well and obviously was in great pain, although she said nothing about that. I lay wretchedly in my bunk, worrying, for I knew how quickly this poisoning could work. It was a matter of great urgency to get her to Suva, for we could find no doctor nearer, and here we were stopped because of bad weather. Within a matter of hours our gay cruise had become a burden, and I wondered if I had made the right decision, or whether I ought to let the ship drive on.

At the first hint of dawn I let draw and continued on our

way. The rain had turned to drizzle, the sky was a uniform grey, the sea angry and white-capped. At noon we got a glimpse of land ahead, blurred and faint; but this proved to be Totoya, recognizable as we passed close south of it in the early afternoon, by reason of the deep bight in its southern side, where the land faded out of sight. The rain was increasing again, reducing visibility to between 1 and 3 miles. But certain of our position now, we altered course direct for Suva, a dead run of 115 miles, Totoya quickly fading into the gloom astern.

All through the night we ran at 5½ knots under the close-reefed mainsail only, the wind reaching gale force in the squalls. There was never a glimpse of a star, the rain persisting, and we ran blind, concentrating on steering an accurate compass course. Susan insisted on standing her share of the watches, and I hated to see her struggling into her oilskins as the motion flung her about the reeling cabin.

Dawn, late in coming, showed no improvement; indeed, the rain was heavier and the wind had not moderated. As navigator I was growing increasingly worried, for the south coast of Viti Levu in the vicinity of Suva is fronted by a barrier reef, and it was vital that we should find the pass leading through it to the safety of the harbour. In other circumstances I would have stopped until the visibility improved, but Susan was getting worse and it was essential to reach medical aid without any further delay. So we continued to drive on. However, I did have something, or so I thought, to console me from the navigational point of view. Running dead before the wind with the mainsail out to port we both knew that in spite of careful steering our tendency was to let the ship come up a trifle to windward (east) of the course. Therefore, when we sighted breakers on the reef, we would have to gybe and steer to the west, keeping within sight of the breakers, and in time we should sight the pass. Nevertheless it was an anxious business.

At 9 a.m. a most providential thing happened. For a few moments, certainly not more than half a minute, the sun shone faintly and I was able to get a hurried snapshot with the sextant. The sun was indistinct, the horizon was close and poorly defined, and on working out the sight I found to my dismay that the resulting position line was 11 miles *west* of the course; yet, as I have said, we both felt convinced we were to the east of the rhumb line. I was in some doubt whether to use the position line or ignore it because of the poor conditions under which the sight had been taken, but acting on the assumption (by no means always correct) that any sight is better than none, I put my trust in it and made the necessary alteration of course for where it indicated Suva pass should lie. The rain closed in on us again, heavier than ever, and I doubted whether we could see a quarter of a mile at times.

Susan in yellow oilskins, against which her face looked very pale, her swollen arm held high across her chest to try to ease the throbbing pain, crouched in the bows, enveloped in rain and spray, straining to see through the murk; for although by account we still had 15 miles to go, it could well be that our latitude was as much in error as our longitude appeared to be, and that we might already be close to the reef.

By 11 o'clock we had run our distance and still could see nothing. We hurried on, expecting to see breakers at any moment. Slowly the apprehensive minutes ticked by.

'Suva Point!' Susan's cry, high and faint, came floating back to me against the wind, as she gestured with her good arm.

And sure enough there it was with houses standing on it, blurred but unmistakable through a temporary gap in the veil of rain. A line of surf lay between it and us, and right ahead stood the two small white towers marking the sides of the pass. Then the rain closed in again, blotting out everything; but we did not care now; our worries were over.

8

Out of the Tropics

We remained for two weeks at Suva, lying off the Royal Suva Yacht Club, where Mossie Ragg, the secretary, did everything he could for us, and each day he drove Susan to the hospital for treatment.

At school many years ago I had been friends with a shy sixth-former, Kenneth Maddocks; we had not met or corresponded since, and now he was Governor of Fiji. He and Lady Maddocks were quicker off the mark than we were, and before I could get up to Government House to sign the book, they sent a car to fetch us up for lunch. For my part the reunion was a great pleasure, but unfortunately it occurred at a difficult time, for our visit coincided with the peak of the Fiji sugar troubles. Over 85 per cent of the growers are Indian, and the attempt to prevent them from cutting the 1960 sugar crop was a racially inspired move which inflamed Indo-Fijian relations; but now the growers were threatening to burn their crops unless the mills agreed to accept all their cane—an impossibility at that late stage. Police and army were ready for quick action should the need arise, and on the evening of the lunch party we listened on the radio to Sir Kenneth, preceded by the national anthem, making a broadcast appeal for saner thinking, his theme being that half a loaf is better than no bread. He and Lady Maddocks came for a short sail in *Wanderer*, when, we like to think, they were able to relax from their worries for a little while, and escape from the burden of being public figures. But even that was partly denied them, as news of their proposed outing had spread, and the Yacht Club, where I picked them

up in the dinghy, was more crowded than I had ever known it
before.

Most people who go to the South Pacific have read such
glowing accounts of the perfection of the islands and the charm
of the people who inhabit them, that there is some risk of
being disappointed by the reality. Many of the islands are
difficult of approach because of the reefs among which they lie;
anchorages tend to be exposed, inconveniently deep, or are
foul with coral heads; and some islands have no anchorages of
any kind. There may be insect pests, awkward landing places,
or inhabitants spoilt by the tourist invasion. But these draw-
backs do not apply to the small islands which lie within the
Great Astrolabe Reef about 40 miles south of Suva. Some of
these are inhabited, and most are easy of approach and lie in
water that is well sheltered except from south-west winds, which
are rare in the fine weather season. With no large rivers to bring
down silt, and no great heights to gather cloud, the water is
crystal clear. Pilotage by eye is easy (except in the bay on the
north-west side of the larger Ono Island), and the colouring
of the reefs is beautiful.

We spent a week inside the reef, stopping first at the island
of Ndravuni, which is only 1 mile long and less than half a
mile across at its widest part; it had a population of sixty, some
of whom had never been even as far as Suva. The Chief invited
us ashore in the evening to a *yanggona* drinking party and to
hear some singing. With the older men of the island we sat
cross-legged on the mat-covered floor of the Chief's house, in a
circle round the *yanggona* bowl, from which the bitter drink was
ladled out in coconut husks. Twelve young men, grouped
closely in a corner of the room, sang in harmony and in descant
to the accompaniment of two guitars. Those songs haunt us
still. In the quieter passages we could hear the cry of a child,
the whine of a dog, and the steady beat of the pestle pounding
the *yanggona* roots. Through the doorway we saw moonlight
gleaming on the palm fronds and drawing their slanting black
shadows sharply on the white beach where the tiny lagoon
waves broke with a whisper. Afterwards the men helped us

carry the dinghy down to the water, and before pushing us off into the night, they loaded the dinghy with gifts of fruit and sang their farewell song, 'Isa Lei'.

Lovely Yaukuve, a little smaller than Ndravuni, we had entirely to ourselves, for it is uninhabited, but there is a tiny palm-frond hut on the beach to shelter those who come occasionally to gather nuts and make copra. For three wonderful days we enjoyed this gem of an island, running about like children on its beaches, where the only footprints were our own; walking through the cool shade of the trees to the windward side to watch the swell breaking on the distant reef. Once we climbed to the top of its 400-ft. hill, forcing our way through stiff, head-high grass, sweating and breathless, for the heat was almost overpowering; and then scrambled quickly down again to plunge into the sea and float over the gorgeously coloured corals where vivid little fish swam in neat formations. Like the other small islands within the reef, Yaukuve has no well or spring water; but that is no real hardship, for it abounds in young drinking nuts, and the palms lean at an angle so accommodating that I was able to climb them, pick the nuts and toss them down to my thirsty woman squatting in the shade beneath.

Then we went on to Mbulia, having first sailed out to have a look at the reef which protects these islands, a reef:

Where the sea-egg flames on the coral and the long-backed breakers croon
Their endless ocean legends to the lazy, locked lagoon.

And so to the larger island of Ono, where the Chief took Susan on a tour of inspection and to gather fruit, while I rowed up the little stream which splits the village, for septic sores on my legs deterred me from taking part in shore excursions.

It was with sadness that on a grey day towards the end of September we left the Great Astrolabe Reef. The islands which lie within its protection surpass anything that can be produced in Technicolor for the movies, and the people who live there are friendly, courteous, and at present quite unspoilt by contact with the outside world. But this cannot last, and already there is talk of 'opening up' these islands as a tourist attraction. We rounded Cape Washington, the western extreme of Kandavu, and headed south towards New Zealand 1,000 miles away.

The weather immediately took a turn for the worse. A night of calm and torrential rain was followed by several days of hard headwinds, and that in a part of the ocean where we might with reason have expected the trade wind to blow in moderation. We left the ship to plunge slowly unattended on her way, though we did keep some sort of a look-out by night, because we had heard that Japanese tuna-fishing vessels were at work with their 5-mile lines to the south of Fiji; but we saw nothing. After we had been at sea for nearly a week we crossed the Tropic of Capricorn, where we picked up a fine fair wind, and under main and spinnaker made the best day's run of the passage, 140 miles. Not until then did the motion become sufficiently regular for Susan to be able to fry our evening meal, which was a great treat after days of pressure-cooked food.

Several days after crossing the tropic we fell in with wandering albatrosses and expended a lot of movie film in an attempt to record their soaring, effortless flight; mostly they remained close to the water, and as they banked steeply on the turn the outermost feathers of the lower wing almost touched the water; often they vanished behind the intervening swell. We offered them some canned New Zealand sausages, but apparently they thought as little of these as we did, giving them merely a scornful glance as they swept by. We never saw them take anything from the sea, but as they live largely on cuttlefish, it is probable that much of their food is obtained during the night when these and other marine creatures come close to the surface. The wandering albatross, with its 10-to-11-ft. wing span, has rarely been seen north of 30° south latitude, and only goes ashore to breed on the smaller islands of the southern ocean.

With the exception of the transit of the Panama canal and a few miles each side of it, we had for the past eleven months been sailing towards the west horizon. It was strange now to be making southing, to find the days rapidly drawing out and with increasing periods of twilight; the air felt crisper as the temperature steadily fell, and the nights became so cool that we were glad to have blankets on our bunks and sweaters and trousers when on watch.

The wind, as was to be expected there, became variable in strength and direction, and often there was rain. Then as we neared New Zealand we learnt from the radio of a cyclonic disturbance centred near Lord Howe Island and expected to travel in our direction. Gale warnings were broadcast.

We had reached a position 115 miles north of Cape Brett (our intended landfall) by the time the anticipated gale arrived. It blew from north-east and was accompanied by heavy and continuous rain. At the beginning we lay-to under the close-reefed mainsail, but very soon there was too much wind for that and we took it in. At that time the anemometer registered 45 knots, a strong gale, but an hour later I guessed the wind speed to be 50 knots, a storm, but did not check this. The sea was a dirty grey-green, more appropriate to the North Atlantic in winter than to the South Pacific in spring, and it smoked as the crests were torn off and driven horizontally to leeward. The rain and spray was driven so hard that it hurt my face when I put my head out of the hatchway, and I could not look to windward without shielding my eyes. The wind howled a savage note in the rigging, and some rope aloft vibrated furiously, shaking the whole ship.

There was no real cause for anxiety. We had plenty of sea-room, and *Wanderer* had come safely through some hard weather in the past. But I was scared by the uncontrolled violence of the wind, and the nagging thought that this could be an out-of-season cyclone; the falling glass and unchanging direction of the wind indicated that we were in the path of the disturbance. We lay in our bunks, I with chattering teeth. Although both of us were suffering from cold feet just then—we had not thought to bring hot-water bottles or bedroom slippers with us—I knew it was not cold that made my teeth chatter. Although she hates bad weather, Susan is less easily disturbed by it than I am, and she spent most of the day dozing, but she turned out to scramble some eggs for supper. I could not sleep, so I read a whodunit, and on turning the last page realized that I had very little idea of what it was all about.

Fortunately the gale did not blow with its full fury for many hours, or the sea would have become dangerous. As it was we did ship some heavy dollops from time to time. One landed so solidly on deck that for a moment the daylight was dimmed, and due presumably to the momentary rise of pressure, the pen of the barograph jumped vertically up and down one-tenth of an inch. At the same time a spurt of water came in through the water-trap ventilator over Susan's bunk, but because of the angle of heel it left her bunk untouched and tumbled into mine. With the low overcast the afternoon was so dark that we had to light the lamps at 4 o'clock, but although we had closed everything except the forward ventilators, they flickered and smoked and sometimes blew out.

Later we learnt that at Cape Brett lighthouse this gale attained a velocity of 75 knots, which was well in excess of my estimated storm, and as we were to windward of the cape it seems reasonable to suppose that we were having much the same kind of weather. Winds exceeding 63 knots are classed as hurricanes.

When it started to moderate the wind dropped quickly, but we waited some hours for the sea to go down before making sail, and then ran on with a huge overtaking swell—which appeared to be exactly what the albatrosses needed for perfect, wing-motionless flight—towards the land. We sighted Cape Brett at breakfast-time on our fourteenth day at sea, and headed in towards the Bay of Islands, which lies to the west of the cape. As we sailed in, the swell slowly lost height and had subsided by the time we reached an anchorage off the brightly painted little town of Russell. The sun then shone, and we spread out on deck some of our wet things to dry.

Within a few minutes of our arrival Doug Lush, a stranger who soon became a friend, rowed off to us with a gift of fresh butter, milk, bread, and the day's paper. Someone else brought an invitation from the hotel-keeper to be his guests for dinner that evening. He was followed by Dick McIlvride, whom we had met at Sydney seven years ago, shortly after his yacht *Gesture* had been dismasted, near Lord Howe Island.

'It's good to see you two again after all this time,' he said as he stepped aboard and almost pulped our hands. 'If you're tired of living afloat, Pat and I will move out of our little house and you can go and stay in it for as long as you like.'

We declined his kind offer, as we feel happier about *Wanderer* at night if we are on board, and Susan said:

'We often wondered about you after we left Sydney. How did the return trip to New Zealand go?'

'Well,' he replied, 'Pat's mother lives in New South Wales, and she was not too happy about the dismasting; she offered to pay Pat's steamship fare back home. But I just laughed and said that kind of thing never happens more than once in a lifetime, so Pat came along with us. The odd thing was, though, we were dismasted again that trip, way out in the Tasman. But we got in all right under jury rig.'

He sold *Gesture* after that (she has since been dismasted for the third time) and bought a handsome American-designed ketch, which he was then preparing for a trip 'up the islands', that is, to Polynesia.

We spent five months in New Zealand, and only sailed 600 miles in all that time, confining our cruising to the pleasant waters which lie between the Bay of Islands and Auckland. But our reasons for going to New Zealand for a second time were to revisit old friends, and get to know a small part of the country and its people well; to give *Wanderer* a refit; and to recuperate after the 15,000-mile voyage out from England, for we were both tired and suffering from the after effects of blood poisoning and nights that were too hot. All those things we did in a most satisfactory manner; indeed, our second visit to the Dominion proved to be even more enjoyable than the first one, and as before, everyone we met was welcoming, kind, and helpful.

In easy stages we made our way south to Auckland, wondering where we would find a berth, for in mid-week at that time of year no doubt all the moorings would be occupied, and

Auckland does not offer a safe and convenient place for a small yacht to drop anchor in. But apparently we had been expected, for as we sailed up the harbour a customs launch ranged alongside and hailed.

'Please go to Westhaven. A berth has been reserved for you there.'

So we continued up the harbour, past the busy docks and the ships lying in the stream waiting for berths at which to discharge cargo or load, towards the graceful curve of the new harbour bridge; just before reaching it we turned to port and entered the walled yacht harbour. The Custodian met us and helped us secure between the only vacant pair of posts, and he and his wife kindly offered us the use of their bath and laundry facilities, and rarely during our stay did we pass their house without receiving some little gift—a newly baked cake, a pie, or a pot of home-made jam.

Our berth was close to the harbour bridge, and we never tired of watching the four lanes of traffic flowing over it swiftly and smoothly, except when someone had a breakdown (it was surprising how often that happened) or stopped at the summit to admire the breath-taking view; then loudspeakers brayed, and a scarlet jeep dashed up from the control station to get the offender started on his way again with the minimum delay. So well is the bridge patronized that the tolls had recently been reduced to 2s. for a car. Cyclists and pedestrians are not permitted to use it.

Since the bridge was built there are no facilities for hauling a yacht out at Westhaven; so for our refit we went to Okahau Bay, a couple of miles east of the city, where the Royal Akarana Yacht Club stands beside the hauling-out area. At Tahiti we had met Tom Blackman, Vice-Commodore of the Akarana, and when one Sunday evening prior to our refit we put in an appearance at the Club, we were made welcome and our needs

PLATE 17
For Christmas week we went to Swansea Bay, Kawau Island, where we arrived in the evening and brought up in the sheltered cove close beside the Lidgards' perfectly situated house.

were immediately taken in hand. A few days later *Wanderer* was hauled out in a cradle which was lent to us, and placed close to the Club House, where we received much help and kindness, particularly from the secretary, Charlie Williams, and his lovable wife.

Susan and I continued to live aboard, and in great comfort, for all the Club facilities were put at our disposal, and bread, milk, groceries, and the daily paper were delivered on board; and when we went ashore to sample the almost continuous stream of hospitality we had only to climb down a ladder instead of making a wet trip in the dinghy. We remained there for three pleasant weeks, and in good weather attended to the refit. But at times it was difficult to get on with the work because of the number of people who came to talk or to offer us meals or drives through the countryside, or who wanted to take us away to live with them for a week or two. Some of these temptations we could not resist, and thanks to our good friend Jack Brooke we were able to see a lot of the North Island. The people who lived in the scenic South Island could not understand why we declined their invitations to go and stay with them; but our time in the Dominion was necessarily limited, and always we prefer to get to know a small part of a country and its people well, rather than catch a fleeting glimpse of a larger area.

While the ship was hauled out we received much practical help from other sailing people, for among the fraternity are men skilled in every branch of boatbuilding and engineering, all eager to assist in any way they could. Susan and I spent most of the daylight hours cleaning, scraping, chipping, rubbing down, and painting and varnishing, and we removed the green deposit from the copper sheathing to expose copper oxide, which provided a new lease of anti-fouling life.

Towards the end of our time ashore *Pambili* (she had arrived in New Zealand some time after us) was hauled out nearby, and it was good to have Roger and Bill—the one fair and lean,

PLATE 18
A buffet Christmas lunch, prepared by Mrs. Lidgard, was eaten on the lawn in the sunshine by a party of thirty-six; all had come by boat.

the other dark and handsome, and both deeply bronzed—as close neighbours. They, like ourselves, had come south to refit, but Tahiti was pulling at them so strongly that for the present the completion of their circumnavigation had been postponed. They were both working long hours at a refrigerator factory, rubbing down parts before painting, so as to earn enough money to enable them to sail back and spend another season among the islands. Although they could afford to spend only the week-ends working on their old ship, they managed to give her a good refit and made a number of improvements to her and her gear. They were spurred on to fresh bursts of energy each time we played for them the tape-recordings we had made of the girls singing aboard *Pambili* while she and *Wanderer* lay at the Papeete waterfront.

Their plans went well. They did earn enough money and they did sail back to Tahiti to enjoy again the island life they loved so well. There they met their old friend Wally Hambuechen, an American scientist, and now a sadly changed man. He had married Delphine, a Polynesian girl, on Rurutu, a high island a little larger than Mangareva, and one of the Tubuai Group, about 300 miles south of Tahiti. But his bride had died a few days after the wedding aboard the schooner which was taking them both to Tahiti. The schooner put back and Delphine was buried on Rurutu.

Months later Wally wished to erect over his bride's grave the tombstone which he had had made in Papeete, and Roger and Bill kindly offered to sail him with it to Rurutu, and then take him on to Rarotonga, as his visa for the French islands would then have expired.

The passage took six days, and they anchored in 6 fathoms off the fringing reef on the lee side of the island, for there is no lagoon there, and as *Pambili*'s auxiliary engine was out of action although much work had been done on it at Tahiti, she could not enter the narrow, sheltered channel through the reef which is used by the schooners.

They were all over at the far side of the island where Delphine's parents lived, when an islander rode over the mountain to tell them that *Pambili* was on the reef. In their absence the wind had shifted through 180 deg., and it seems that the ship, in swinging round, had fouled a coral head with her anchor chain, and snubbing on the shortened cable as the sea got up, had parted it and driven ashore. Roger and Bill on horseback galloped across the island, and a dreadful sight greeted them as the reef came into view. Their ship, which had brought them so ably half-way round the world in fair weather and foul, the ship in which they had lived so happily and held their gay parties, lay on her beam ends, and was being lifted by each breaker and smashed down again and again on the sharp coral. Wading out they found the sea washing in and out of her devastated cabin, and such of their personal belongings as had not been smashed or washed away were damaged or destroyed by water, and they were left with little more than the shorts they were wearing.

Hundreds of Rurutans went to their help. Palms were felled, and with these under the wreck, it was rolled further up the reef until it was just outside the reach of the breakers; but by that time there was nothing at all left of the starboard side, and the deck had been almost levered off. Repairs were quite out of the question, so they sold the wreck, including spars, rigging, and sails, to the Chief for £36, and after remaining as guests for a month, returned to Tahiti by schooner.

The story of their fine voyage, which until then had passed almost unnoticed by the Press, now became headline news, as is usually the way when disaster strikes. A reporter on a Sunday paper flew out from England, bought the story for £500, and wrote it up in the required style with heavy emphasis on free love with Tahitian *vahines*, to the dismay of Bill and Roger and the horror of their parents. The two then adopted the Tahitian outlook: when something bad has happened it is best forgotten. So they set about the simple and enjoyable business of spending the money in Tahiti, and it is good to know that their misfortune has not deterred them from seeking further adventure; I have recently heard that they are planning to build a replica of a twin-hull Polynesian canoe—complete with sails of woven pandanus—in which to attempt the long trip to the Hawaiian Islands.

By the time we had got *Wanderer* afloat again Christmas was approaching, and as most of our friends were going away for the long summer holiday we decided to do the same. Naturally enough we went for Christmas week to our favourite anchorage in Swansea Bay, Kawau Island, 30 miles from Auckland, where we arrived in the evening and brought up in the sheltered cove close beside Roy and Mum Lidgard's perfectly situated house. Christmas Day was warm and cloudless, and a number of other craft had arrived; there were presents for everyone and a superb buffet lunch prepared by Mum Lidgard, and eaten by thirty-six people on the lawn which slopes gently down from the house to the water's edge. All had come by boat, and we were their guests.

Some weeks earlier we had given an illustrated talk to 450 members of the Royal Akarana Yacht Club, and I, perhaps unwisely, had said that after visiting a great many islands we still regarded Moorea as the most beautiful island that we knew. Several of the people who spoke to me after the show, referring to this remark, said: 'Then obviously you have never visited our Great Barrier Island.' To complete our education we therefore sailed out to that island, 30 miles seaward, a few days after Christmas, and, making our way through narrow Governor Pass, where one's freshwater tanks can be filled at a convenient waterfall, came into Port Fitzroy, a magnificent natural harbour about 3 miles long and over a mile wide, with a variety of bays and coves from which to select an anchorage. We spent six days there, but failed to work up much enthusiasm for the island itself, covered as it largely is with bush and scrub, through which walking is difficult, and with its lack of good beaches. But we did enjoy the jolly company of many sailing and power-boat people. Each cove and bay had its gathering of craft—there must have been sixty or seventy in or around Port Fitzroy—and there was much coming and going, for everyone but ourselves was busy fishing; indeed, there was such a glut of fish, from whitebait to crayfish, that people ate little else, and smoked what they could not consume, or unloaded on us.

New Year's Eve was a particularly jolly occasion, for our anchorage was shared by the Commodore and Vice-Commodore of the Royal New Zealand Yacht Squadron and the Vice-Commodore of the Royal Akarana Yacht Club, as well as many others, and I felt that my own flag as Vice-Commodore of the Royal Cruising Club was in excellent company. The Squadron is very conscious of flag etiquette, and after the casual behaviour of people at home, it was a pleasure to see all the ensigns come fluttering down together as the Commodore's sunset cannon boomed across the bay, echoing from one shore to the other and back again.

After the Christmas holiday we returned with most of the other yachts to Auckland, putting in at Coromandel and Waihike Island, where we met other old friends, including Pete and Jane Taylor, who had sailed out to New Zealand with Tom and Ann Worth in *Beyond* seven years before, and settled happily there. The last night of our stay at Auckland produced a rather grand occasion. Jimmy Faire, Commodore of the Squadron, had asked me to give an illustrated talk about our voyage from home to members of the Squadron.

'Gladly,' I said, 'but I must have Susan as my projectionist, for we show 300 slides, and I'm sure nobody else would be able to put them on the screen as fast as I need them.'

I knew this would create a problem, for except on the occasion of the annual cocktail party, women are not permitted to set foot inside the Squadron building. But that did not worry Jimmy.

'I will exercise the divine right of Commodores,' he said, and to make the evening a little less embarrassing for Susan, the three flag officers' wives were invited to come along to hold her hand. This we feared might be the thin edge of a wedge which members' wives had been longing to fashion; but we have since learnt that, unruffled, the Squadron has continued in its monastic tradition, and that Susan's is still the only feminine signature in the visitors' book.

On our way north from Auckland we put in at Whangarei to have a tooth attended to, and then learnt why so many yachts have ended their voyages there. Up the river close to the bridge and 15 miles inland, boats lie moored between posts, where they gently take the soft mud each tide. The berth is so sheltered that the wind blows only softly, and the stream has little strength; a water tap and shops are only a few yards away, and one soon falls into the sleepy tenor of the place and grows idle. The longer one remains the more repugnant becomes the thought of the rough and tumble of the open sea.

However, while *Wanderer* lay there we did see something of the soft, green countryside, for Noel and Jean Percy took us away to have a look at their dairy farm, where they were milking eighty-six Jersey cows. New Zealand is essentially a practical, 'do it yourself' country, and labour costs are high, so the entire farm was run with the help of only one man, a share milker. The milk went straight from the milking machine to the separator, from which the cream was run into a churn ready to be collected by the butter-making factory; the skim milk was piped downhill from the separator to the pig sties. The smells of the farm, of grass and pigs and cow dung, came sweetly to our seagoing nostrils. We also visited the Oxborrows' sheep farm near the mouth of the harbour. Since last we were there they had cleared more land, and they now own 5 miles of coastline, including a well-sheltered little harbour called The Nook. They employ no labour, Jim and his son Bill doing all that is needed to look after 2,000 sheep, but professionals are employed for the shearing. They were mustering at the time of our visit, and a beautiful sight the flock was as the dogs moved it over the brow of a hill and down towards the pens, fluid and golden against the bright blue sky, like a gentle wave flowing over a beach; away to one side the waters of the harbour sparkled.

Our last days in New Zealand were spent in or near the Bay of Islands, a delightful miniature cruising ground. Of the many islands there, Motuarohia, 5 miles from Russell, is perhaps the most beautiful, and certainly the most historic. It is 1 mile

long, rises to a height of 275 ft., and is almost split into three by
two lagoons; indeed, in the winter, when the north-east gales
wash the beach away, it is so split, but always joins up again.
On the northern, seaward, side are cliffs and rocks on which
the swell breaks heavily at times; but the southern side has two
clean bays, the eastern one providing the anchorage. Much
of the island is planted with young pines, but there are grassy
slopes where Hereford cattle graze, and little streams.

On Wednesday, 29 November 1769, Cook came here in
Endeavour, and I quote from his journal giving his reasons for
doing so:

> Fresh gales at N.W. and W.N.W., kept plying to windward
> until 7 a.m., and finding that we lost ground every board
> we made, I thought I could not do better than to bear up
> for the bay which lies to the westward of Cape Brett, it
> being at this time not above two leagues to leeward of us,
> for by putting in there we should gain some knowledge of it,
> on the contrary, by keeping the sea with a contrary wind we
> were sure of meeting nothing new.

He anchored south-west of Motuarohia, but grounding
almost immediately on the spit which runs out from the island's
southern shore, berth was shifted a little to the east to a position
just outside the anchorage we used. Landing on the beach with
Banks, Solander, and a party of seamen, Cook was met by and
had a slight brush with between 200 and 300 Maoris, many of
whom had come in canoes from the mainland.

Today the only inhabitants are Colonel and Mrs. Browne,
who own the island. We had called on them during our earlier
voyage when they were just starting with their own hands to
build their house on the flat ground at the eastern end of the
bay in which Cook landed. Seven years later they recognized
Wanderer as she approached the anchorage, and hoisted a welcoming signal on their flagstaff. So as soon as we had anchored
and stowed the sails, we landed on the smooth beach of shells
and fine shingle in front of the now completed house. Bill and
Myra met us and helped carry the dinghy up. Their welcome

was sincere and touching, and soon we were at our ease in their long, comfortable living-room, which has landscape windows giving fine views of the anchorage, the western part of the island and the nearest lagoon, and through a gap a glimpse of the Ninepin, a remarkable black pinnacle rock 5 miles away. We sat and talked for a while of many things, then a walk up through the firs and a climb to the top of the hill where the Maoris had their *pa* (stronghold) in Cook's day gave us a proper appetite for the dinner Myra cooked on her fircone-fired kitchen range. Lamplight gleamed softly on the old oak furniture and on the polished brass and copper, just as it would in an old-established English home, and during the brief lulls in the conversation we could hear the faint brush of small waves breaking on the shingle, and the occasional boom as a blowhole on the cliffy, seaward side of the island spouted.

Afterwards, while Myra and Susan were washing up, Bill said to me:

'Myra and I are very worried about Susan. You've chosen to go home the hard way, but I served for some years in Egypt and I know a lot about the Red Sea; I can tell you it's no place for a small sailing craft at any time of year, and it would be tragic if Susan had another go of blood poisoning there.'

The same thought had occurred to me, and I said so; but Susan is a very determined person.

'If you're set on going through with this,' Bill continued, 'surely you could find a male companion, and Myra and I would just love to have Susan here and look after her until it's time for her to join you in the Med.'

After we had got into our bunks that night I told Susan what he had said.

'I know,' she replied. 'Myra had a go at me while we were in the kitchen. Bless them both, they are a couple of dears to be so worried; but if you go up the Red Sea, and I think you

PLATE 19
Motuarohia from the hill on which the Maoris had their *pa*, showing the lagoons which almost split the island into three, and the beach where Captain Cook landed. The Brownes' house stands just beyond the far lagoon.

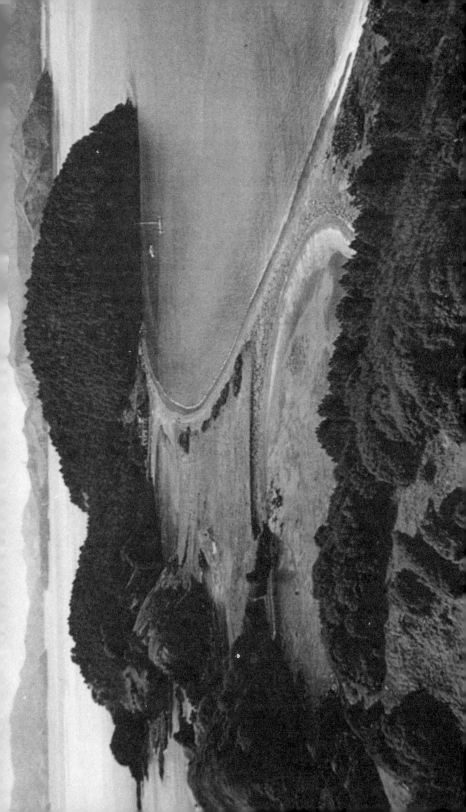

must to get it out of your system, then I'm coming too. I told Myra that, and I think she understands.'

Living on a small island without other inhabitants certainly has its glamorous side, but it calls for the kind of practical ability and self-reliance which everyone does not possess. The Brownes have a radio transmitter and can order their stores to be sent out from Russell in one of Fuller's ferry boats employed on the 'cream run', a round of the islands and neighbouring coast. But on arrival everything has to be trans-shipped into a dinghy, brought ashore, and carried up the beach, and this includes heavy items such as drums of fuel for the electric generating and water-pumping plant. Fircones for the kitchen range have to be gathered, and a watch kept on summer picnic parties, which by careless smoking or lighting fires might destroy the fir plantations. The garden, too, needs attention, and so do the fatting cattle occasionally. But in spite of all this Bill, who is a retired Sapper, had found time to do a considerable amount of survey work in his own small boat along the north-east coast of New Zealand, and when the new Admiralty chart of the area is published, his name will appear on it.

While we lay at Motuarohia we had news of three cyclones which were then on the move in the South-Western Pacific. One of them, close to New Caledonia, wrecked two ships and caused salvage operations on the *Runic* (she had been aground on Middleton Reef for the past month) to be abandoned. The second, farther to the east, destroyed half of the buildings on Vava'u in the Tonga Group, and did an estimated £200,000 worth of damage; we felt anxious about the people we had met there, particularly the hymn-singing girls and their teachers. The third cyclone passed near the Cook Islands, but apparently caused no serious damage.

PLATE 20
One morning in the Coral Sea the Swedish ship *Tenos*, lifting and falling majestically on the long swell, altered course to close and speak with us. She was the first ship we had seen out of sight of land since leaving Panama, and this chance meeting quite made our day.

9

The Coral Sea

The day was overcast when we sailed away from the Bay of Islands bound towards Nouméa, 900 miles away in the big French island of New Caledonia; there was drizzle and a moderate beam wind. We felt sad at leaving our many friends behind, and as we reached past Motuarohia and out towards the Ninepin, we cast many a backward glance at the Brownes' little white house which peeped out at us across the lagoon between Middle and East Islands, for there we had spent some of our happiest moments.

As we increased our distance from the land (it vanished before nightfall) the wind freshened, and we learnt from the radio that a deep depression had formed south of Fiji; we wondered anxiously which way it would move, for depressions forming in that latitude can develop into cyclones. The five degree square in which we were sailing was liable to 10 per cent of gales, and as we reduced sail we realized that once again we were in for a spell of bad weather, just as on all our previous passages in the South-West Pacific. The following evening found us hove-to in an easterly gale. The past five months of soft living in New Zealand had done nothing to prepare us for this, and we both felt sick and depressed.

The same conditions with rain continued until the following evening, when the wind reached 45 knots; this was too much for the small amount of sail we had set, so we took it in and lay a-hull for the next 30 hours. Sights were not possible, and as the wind moderated a trifle at dawn of our fourth day out, and we feared that we might have been set towards the unlit Three

Kings, which lie north of New Zealand, we set the staysail and steered the course with the gale on the starboard quarter. At something over 6 knots that was exciting sailing, too exciting at times, for a heavy sea was running, and as is usual in such weather there occurred at frequent intervals a succession of seas steeper and higher than the others. For these it was wise to bear right away so as to take them stern-on. Both sea and sky were a dismal grey; the rain never ceased for a moment; the great shouting wind roared in our ears, and the bow-wave creamed high on either side.

The staysail alone had little steadying effect, and down in the cabin the motion seemed to be particularly violent and jerky, and although Susan had stowed the food lockers with her usual care, some of their contents had worked loose and crashed from side to side as the ship rolled. Everything below was damp and sticky to the touch, and drops of spray, which had entered while the hatch was open for a moment as Susan and I changed places at the helm, clung to bulkheads, deckhead, and furniture. We had shipped the washboards in the companionway, and through the perspex window in the upper one I could see Susan, her bare legs straddling the cockpit, her body in its gleaming yellow oilskin swaying to the motion. There was a firm look of competent concentration on her face, down which the rain was running, and a wisp of auburn hair, escaped from the confines of her sou'wester, blew across it. I knew the ship was in good hands and, mentally, I could relax. But I was not below for long, as steering needed one's full attention, so we took only short spells at the helm; even so by late afternoon we were growing tired, and in a moment of inattention I let the ship round up, bringing the sea abeam at one of those times when a succession of particularly heavy seas were overtaking us. Poor *Wanderer* took the top of one of these aboard over her full length. It buried her so that only the upturned dinghy amidships and the four white ventilating cowls on the coachroof were visible, and for a few seconds she felt waterlogged and sluggish as I clung on thigh deep in the overflowing cockpit. Clearly the time had come to stop this wild career before something serious happened; so Susan took the helm while I handed the staysail, and then we ran on more sedately under bare poles.

To our great relief the wind moderated in the night, and little by little we made sail; but the rain continued, and there was much lightning with heavy rolls of thunder. The sea was remarkably phosphorescent, not with the usual sparkling light but with a general all-over luminosity. Each time the lee side deck was invaded by a crest, the wetted area glowed for as long as a minute with a pale green milkiness, just as though it had received a coat of luminous paint.

During our fifth day at sea the sun came out, and we were able to open the ports and hatches and get some of our wet things out to air; but the humidity was still so high that nothing dried. Our appetites returned and we ate enormously of the many good things that had been given to us in New Zealand. There followed a day of glorious sailing when the fresh beam wind gave us a run of 144 miles. But when the wind hauled round to head us off and again freshened we hove-to once more and waited for a change, and when that came we got the ship to steer herself close-hauled in the right direction. The radio news mostly concerned a Russian who had made a journey into space. Looking at the myriad stars that night, the matter seemed of small significance in relation to the universe.

The island of New Caledonia is about 200 miles long in a north-west—south-east axis, and is enclosed by the second longest coral reef formation in the world. This reef, much of which is sunken, extends for a distance of 40 miles south of the main island, and as it interferes with the flow of the south-east trade-wind drift, the currents in its vicinity are variable and strong; indeed, *Pacific Islands Pilot*, Vol. II, defines a large area outside the reef as being unsafe for navigation because of those currents. We were bound for Boulari Pass—the best entrance in the reef to the lagoon and the port of Nouméa, which lies on the south-west side of the island. The pass is 45 miles north-west of the southern extremity of the reef, and we considered it desirable to make our landfall on the reef itself some distance south-east of the pass in order to be sure of reaching the pass, for if we steered direct for it the current might sweep us by, and it would then be difficult, or perhaps impossible, to beat back. This entailed sailing through the dangerous area. While we were still some 80 miles from the pass we encountered a south-west setting current of nearly 1 knot, and having obtained good observations with which to fix our position, we dared to approach by night to within 10 miles of the reef, and there hove-to until daylight. We kept a sharp look-out for breakers, and had several scares when we drifted through areas of over-falls. At dawn we let draw and soon sighted a ship on the starboard bow; she seemed to be very steady and fixed in position, and as we drew closer we saw that this was a wreck, one of several which are hard and fast on that reef and out of sight of land except in very clear weather. Bringing forward a position line obtained from a dawn sight of Rigel Kent (one of the Southern Cross pointers) and crossing it with one from the sun, we found that we were a long way ahead of our reckoning and that the south-west current had overnight changed to a north-west direction and had increased in velocity. We understood then the force of the warning in the *Pilot*, yet we could have made our approach in no other satisfactory way.

There was little wind that day and we did not come up with Boulari Pass until nightfall. However, the pass and the channel which leads from it for 15 miles among the reefs and islands of the lagoon to the port of Nouméa are well lighted, and we had little difficulty in making our way through it to the port, where we crept cautiously into a dark, well-sheltered bay just south of the town, and anchored. We were fortunate to have got in when we did, for during the night heavy rain set in and continued for 24 hours, reducing visibility to less than a mile.

In going to Nouméa we had hoped to find a second Papeete, but were disappointed. The squalid town held few attractions for us, and seemed scarcely to have recovered from the time when there was a big penal settlement there. But in those days at least it could boast some strange characters, such as the famous French violinist who murdered his wife's lover, cut out his heart and cooked it, and gave it to his wife for dinner. For years he could be seen and heard leading the convicts' orchestra in the rotunda of a Nouméa hotel. We were most fortunate in meeting the Reid family. Earl, a New Zealander, worked for the South Pacific Commission, which has its headquarters at Nouméa; his wife, Leila, is from Australia. They and their young family—the boys were at a French school, and they spoke the language so well that not until there was a French guest in the house did Earl and Leila realize the shocking nature of their speech—made us so welcome that we could walk into their house (from which there is a fine view of the harbour) at any time and feel we were wanted. They showed us something of the island, which looks fertile but seems to grow little of commercial value, its chief export today being nickel. We also visited the aquarium, where there is some coral from the nearby reef, which after being exposed to ultra-violet light, glows beautifully with vivid colour for a time in the darkened gallery.

After several days with much heavy rain, we left to sail northwest inside the reef to see a little more of the island, and to visit St. Vincent Bay some 30 miles away. We had expected to do our pilotage by eye, which is the usual method of reef navigation in clear water; but we had not reckoned with the rain, which had washed so much soil into the lagoon that the water was thick and brown just as we had found it in the Demerara River, and therefore we could not see the dangers. Sailing at high speed with a fresh, fair wind among the shoals and reefs and little islands was rather too exciting, and twice we passed uncomfortably close to uncharted rocks which were visible only because they had no more than a few inches of water over them. But in the evening we came safely to an anchorage in the lee of a small island in St. Vincent Bay. With about 60 sq. miles of sheltered water and a dozen low, green islands framed by the magnificent chain of mountains which forms the backbone of New Caledonia, their peaks rising to between 2,000 and 5,000 ft., it is an attractive little cruising ground. With a mass of disordered cirrus, such as we have often seen before the onset of bad weather, the sky looked so un-

healthy that we remained in the bay for two more nights, finding anchorage in a well-sheltered cove on the north coast of
uninhabited Ducos Island, which is hilly with rough sheep
pasture, and pleasant to walk over; but the mosquitoes were so
persistent at night that we had to rig nets over our bunks.
Embedded in the rock outcrops on all parts of the island, even
on top of the hills, we found quantities of seashells.

Bound for Port Moresby in Papua–New Guinea, we had to
sail across 1,300 miles of the Coral Sea, which even in these
days of radar and other aids is regarded as hazardous navigation, for it contains many coral reefs and low islets, and the
extensive blank areas on the charts show that much of it yet
has to be surveyed. The chart of the reef anchorages is based
largely on the survey made by Captain H. M. Denham in
H.M.S. *Herald* in 1860, and bears the following inscription:

> These plans and a masthead look-out will enable a ship to
> round to under the lee of the reefs where (as under the Ply-
> mouth breakwater) she may caulk topsides, set up rigging,
> rate chronometers, obtain turtle, fish and seafowl eggs. On
> some of the more salient reefs beacons were erected by Capt.
> Denham, and for the sake of castaways, cocoa-nuts, shrubs,
> grasses, and every description of seed likely to grow, were
> sown in the way to promote the superstructure; and it is
> most desirable that these refuge-spots should be held sacred
> for universal benefit and not ruthlessly destroyed by the
> guano-seeker.

After reading this we would have liked to have a look at
one of those islets, and perhaps spend a night in its lee; but we
did not do so, for although such a venture has to be attempted
occasionally during a world voyage, a small yacht is not well
suited to the purpose. Unless she has spent the night in the
near neighbourhood, and that would be dangerous because of
the unpredictable currents, which near the reefs can attain a
rate of 3 knots, she will probably not travel fast enough to find
it while the sun is still sufficiently high to permit her to be
conned safely to an anchorage; for if one fails to get a set of

star sights at dawn—that cannot be depended upon because of the short twilight in the tropics and the chance of cloud—it may well be impossible to fix the position accurately until noon. Also, from deck level these low islets are only visible for a short distance, and the height of eye is limited because the motion of the small vessel makes it impossible to go sufficiently high up the mast, or to remain aloft for any length of time.

To start with we sailed on a westerly course for 50 miles to make a good offing from the barrier reef of New Caledonia. From that point, and to avoid most of the Coral Sea dangers, we steered north-west for 220 miles to pass between two vigias: 'Reef reported 1946' and 'Discoloured water'. There we altered course a little more northerly to pass east of another vigia, and after that were able to steer direct for Hood Point, our intended Papua–New Guinea landfall.

At last we seemed to have escaped from the bad weather which had dogged us for so long, and for the first time in many months *Wanderer* loped along with an easy, swinging motion, and averaged 110 miles a day for the first week. But the trip was remarkable in that we had rain, often heavy, during some part of nearly every day. At the point where we altered course direct for Papua, we were able to set the twins and get the ship to steer herself while we took a holiday. After the first night in our bunks we found the deck scattered with flying fish—two had even come into the cabin by way of the forehatch—and Susan fried them for breakfast; they were delicious. It has often been said that a light attracts these beautiful little creatures, and it is true that we had the riding light burning that night; but we always do show a light when neither of us is on deck, yet it is rare indeed for *Wanderer* to have such a miraculous draught of fishes, and only on a few occasions during the entire voyage have there been sufficient of them to make a dish.

The pleasant self-steering interlude was interrupted by a tiresome 30-knot wind, which caused the ship to sheer several points away each side of the course, so that first one sail then the other shook angrily. This was not only bad for our nerves, but bad for the sails, so we took them in and ran on under trysail, re-setting the twin as soon as the trade wind recovered its manners.

One morning while I was cooking breakfast and Susan was in the cockpit doing her hair, she noticed a ship crossing our wake in a northerly direction a mile or so away. The ship held her course until almost out of sight, then turned, came back, and slowly overhauled us. By the time she was abeam about 100 yards away, and with engines stopped, she was proceeding at exactly our own speed, and she remained with us for several minutes, lifting and falling majestically on the long swell. Her name was *Tenos*, a Swedish ship of the Australia-West Pacific Line, handsome and immaculate, probably bound for Hong Kong. Her master hailed us through a megaphone, but *Wanderer* made so much noise as she bustled importantly along, that we were unable to hear all he said; but we understood him to ask if we were all right, and to offer us anything of which we might be in need. Today the sailing-ship routes are so empty that this was the first ship we had seen when out of sight of land since leaving Panama, and the meeting, by giving us something fresh to think and talk about, quite made our day; but we were sorry when *Tenos*, having wished us a good voyage, went on her way to leave us in the empty ocean with a sundog in her place.

As we approached Papua we fell in with the outskirts of a cyclonic disturbance. An overcast sky and heavy rain prevented us from getting any sights, and as we did not care to approach the barrier reef, which in places lies as many as 15 miles from the shore, without being certain of our position, we hove-to and remained so for the best part of three days. The weather was particularly hot and humid, and we were in a sorry state. Most things below were damp, including our clothes and bedding; there was the warm, frowsty smell of mildew in the cabin, and we ourselves felt so unclean that we washed all over in fresh water; but because of the motion that was a major undertaking, and the wash-bowl had to be chocked up at just the right angle to prevent the water from being flung out of it when the ship lurched to leeward; of course, the towels were wet and smelly, too.

On the third day I managed to get a snapshot of the tired and bleary sun, and this made it clear that, unexpectedly, we had been set away from the coast by a 1-knot current, whereas all the available information suggested that the current would be setting in a north-westerly direction, that is, with the wind. The rain having stopped by then, we moved on again, heading for Basilisk Passage, the entry through the barrier reef to Port Moresby.

The sky at sunset presented a most remarkable sight. Stained orange and purple above the low, black, heavy cloud mass, it resembled a gigantic bruise. As the light on Hood Point has a range of 14 miles, and as the reef extends at least 15 miles west of it, we naturally did not go close enough to sight the light; instead we gave the whole dangerous corner a wide berth. In the early hours of the morning of our fifteenth day at sea we sighted the loom of Port Moresby's lights on the low cloud canopy, and before dawn picked up the 24-mile flashing light, which is one of a pair to lead ships through the pass.

Dawn was almost as remarkable as the sunset had been, and again the predominant colours were orange and purple. Ahead and to starboard lay the great land mass of Papua–New Guinea, but most of its near, low-lying part was buried in mist, long grey rolls of it like dirty cottonwool. Little imagination was needed to visualize the swamps with their snakes and mosquitoes, the villages on stilts above the mud and sand flats of the coast, the heat, the humidity, the fever. Beyond the unhealthy banks of mist towered the ramparts of the Owen Stanley range, clear-cut against a lagoon-green gash in the northern sky.

We came up with Basilisk Passage in the forenoon, and before midday were at anchor off the clean, compact little town of Port Moresby; and scarcely had we squared up on deck than rain, so heavy that it was almost suffocating, came deluging down. May is the beginning of the dry season, and as the port doctor and customs officer hastened to point out, this weather was unheard of, for it *never* rains in May. As Muhlhauser discovered during his circumnavigation in *Amaryllis*, local weather is never quite what it used to be.

We received much kindness from members of the Yacht Club, and other people too numerous to mention individually. (The first time we had Sunday lunch at the Club the raffle was rigged so that we, who had not even bought tickets, won the chicken salad.) We made several visits to Hanuabada, a great village built on stilts out over the shallow water on the fringing reef—most coastal villages are arranged like that, originally as a measure of protection against the marauding tribes from the hills—and each house had its canoe beneath or alongside. We watched some of the outrigger racing canoes, said to be among the fastest sailing craft in the world, skimming across the lagoon, and of course we went to the floating village of Koki, where the people live aboard platform canoes called *lakatois*; each is a permanent residence for a family, the sails being spread on ridgepoles to make an awning. Friends showed us the rubber plantations where the 'boys' get paid about 1*s*. a day, and are happy with that, for it enables them during their 18-month indenture to save enough to buy the bird of paradise feathers which are necessary when obtaining a wife. It took a little time for us to get used to doing our shopping in markets and shops where many of the women wore nothing except a short grass skirt and a lot of tattooing; it was even more surprising to be waited on at dinner in the homes of our friends by girls wearing nothing at all above the waist.

A highlight of our visit was the meeting with our English friend Frank Eyre; one-time Vice-President of the Little Ship Club, he now runs the Australian branch of my publishers, and had flown up from Melbourne on business, timing his arrival with considerable skill to coincide with ours. Susan and I have become so used to our slow mode of transport that as Frank sat down to breakfast with us aboard we found it hard to realize that he had left his home only the previous evening.

We would have liked to remain much longer than the two and a half weeks which was all we could allow ourselves, and to have seen more of that strange country which Australia administers so ably; a country where 500 different languages are spoken, where the roads from the towns penetrate less than

100 miles inland (after that you fly or walk), where villages still stand isolated on the ranges, and where occasionally a ritual murder takes place. One of these, the throat-cutting of a willing martyr, was committed in the presence of a bishop during our stay, and apparently was done in all sincerity from religious motives.

Our reason for hurrying away was the need for us to keep our dates with the seasons on the long homeward voyage, an important one being the passage of the Red Sea in January. To reach the Indian Ocean from Port Moresby we had to pass through the Great North-East Channel which leads to Torres Strait, a particularly difficult stretch of water, for the tidal streams run hard and the whole area is a maze of coral reefs and small islands. We wished to pass through it at neaps, when the tides would be running at their weakest, and we therefore timed our arrival to coincide with the waning moon, expecting Torres Strait to have spring tides a day or two after the full and change, like other places in the world. But in this supposition we were wrong, for at one entrance to the strait tides are springs, while at the other they are neaps, and at certain phases of the moon it is high water at one end while it is low water at the other. This was something we discovered only as we did our homework on the way across the Gulf of Papua. Indeed, so complicated are the tides in that area that the *Admiralty Tide Tables* include data for three standard ports within a space of only 20 miles—Goods Island, Thursday Island, and Twin Island.

The Great North-East Channel runs from Bramble Cay, which marks its north-east end, in a south-westerly direction for 130 miles to Torres Strait.

We had a pleasant trip in remarkably smooth water across to the neighbourhood of Bramble Cay, and hove-to an hour before dawn on the second day out, for although the cay was by account 20 miles ahead, we thought it likely that a west-setting current might be setting us towards it, and we had no wish to get swept past. Susan got a dawn observation of Venus, and this placed us on a line only 5 miles east of the cay; and sure enough as the sun rose there it was, its lattice-work light struc-

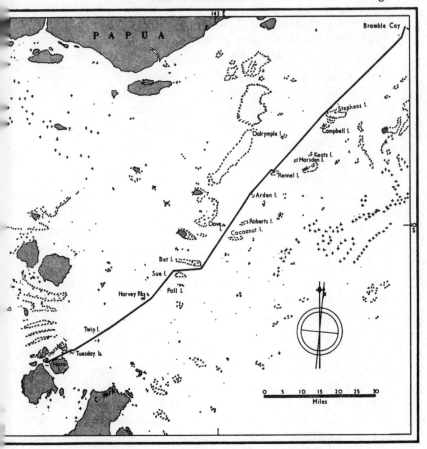

THE GREAT NORTH-EAST CHANNEL

ture showing up clearly in the low light, yet strangely enough we had seen no sign of the 14-mile light itself during the hours of darkness.

I then made a foolish mistake. For some reason which I do not now remember, I thought the best thing was to anchor in the lee of the cay and start the intricate pilotage of the Great North-East Channel at first light next day, instead of continuing the same day, as we ought to have done, for we could then easily have reached an anchorage at Stephens Island only 30 miles on. So we worked up under the lee of the cay, and anchored as close in as we dared to go in 21 fathoms of discoloured water (probably due to silt carried out to sea from the Fly River), using one of our two 35-lb. plough anchors with 10 fathoms of chain and 30 fathoms of nylon warp, and we buoyed the anchor.

Bramble Cay is only a speck of land 10 ft. high and about 300 yds. in diameter. Finding so small a target is not easy, and many navigators have spent many anxious hours searching for it, more especially in the days before a light was established on it. Composed of sand and shells on a coral foundation, it has a depression in the centre where thousands of terns and boobies nest on a patch of coarse grass. Many reefs lie near by, but there is no land within sight, and rarely have we stopped at a place providing such an air of isolation. It was too rough to land, and we spent the rest of the day and the night rolling heavily in the swell, for the cay is too small to offer good shelter. We watched the cloud of birds wheeling and soaring over it, listening to their incessant cries, and at times got gusts of the hot, chicken-house stench from the nesting ground.

Before dawn we shortened in and tried to weigh, but apparently the anchor or the chain had fouled a rock or coral head, and we could not budge it. We sailed and then we motored in every direction in turn, paying out and heaving in the warp, hoping to break the anchor out or draw it clear, but with no success. So we hove in short on the buoy rope and made it fast; *Wanderer*, lifting on the swell, snubbed on the rope ($1\frac{1}{8}$ in. terylene) and it parted where it had been made fast to the ring on the back of the anchor. With raw hands after two hours' work, we realized that there was nothing more we could do, so we abandoned the anchor, cutting the warp and losing 10 fathoms of that as well as the chain.

'Poor old Coldnose,' said Susan as we sailed away. 'I feel as though I've left a bit of myself there at Bramble Cay.'

'If we have to anchor on coral again and lose the other one,' I replied, 'we really will become a Flying Dutchman.'

Although, of course, every long-distance yacht ought to carry a third anchor, we had never been able to find room for it. Now we carry four.

With our sails hard curved by the fresh beam wind, we then hurried away to the south-west and soon raised the first of the small, gleaming, palm-clad islands: Stephens, Campbell, Dalrymple, Keats, and Marsden went flashing by as we tore along at just under 7 knots, carrying the single-reefed mainsail and large staysail. That afternoon we came to an anchorage on a sandy bottom in 4 fathoms close to the fringing reef of un-inhabited Rennel Island. Sheltered from the rushing wind for the first time that day, we bathed and relaxed, and Susan combed the salt out of her long hair.

After the discomforts of Bramble Cay we had a wonderfully sleepful night, and were on our way at dawn. There was a little more wind that day, so with the reefed mainsail we carried the small staysail, and again made our maximum speed with the wind just forward of the beam. In turn Arden, Roberts, and Cocoanut Islands flashed by to port, and Dove Island to starboard, all perfect examples of coral islands with gleaming golden beaches and leaning palms, wind-slashed and sun-drenched, each with a snow-white line of breakers on its windward side. The sea was an almost impossible colour, such as may sometimes be found in a shallow lagoon with a clean sand bottom, a dazzling turquoise without a blemish, except where the occasional orange sea-snake writhed near the surface, and the purple shadows of the small, fleecy clouds went romping across it; these, when seen suddenly from out of the corner of one's eye, gave a momentary impression that a reef lay there.

On we sped, for a short time out of sight of land, for the islands are low and soon dip below the horizon. Then we sighted the thin beacon on Bet Reef, rounded it, slashed past Bet, Sue, and Poll Islands (the captain's three daughters?), and were temporarily out in the clear again. The wind by then was blowing at something over 30 knots. Fairly smooth though the water was, the spray flew in sheets, the sun painting rainbows in the bow wave, and drying the spray on us and the ship almost as quickly as it fell, leaving everything covered with a gritty rime. This was sailing at its very best; we could not have been more fortunate in our conditions for this tricky channel, and

the time flew. Harvey Rocks came next, and by then the afternoon was well advanced, and we began to wonder where we
would find an anchorage for the night. Possibly the next speck
of land, Twin Island, would serve, but as there was still more
than an hour of daylight to go when we reached it, we rushed on
for another 8 miles and came to the Tuesday Islets, Nos. 1, 2,
3, and 4—after such a galaxy of islands the early explorers must
have been getting short of names—and although the shelter did
not look very promising, we had to stop, for there was no other
anchorage this side of Thursday Island, which lay 8 miles
farther on. Night would be upon us shortly, and the shallow
passage leading to Thursday Island anchorage is not lighted.
We therefore shot in as close under the islets' lee as we dared to
go, dropped our only remaining anchor in 3 fathoms, veered
20 fathoms of cable, rigged a nylon spring on that, and hoped
for the best.

The night was a miserable one, for the wind veered a little
and we were then not properly sheltered by the islets; we
pitched and rolled horribly, expecting any moment to have to
get under way; but our anchor held manfully. How glad we
were when daylight brought the anchor watches to an end and
allowed us to continue to Thursday Island, where we anchored
off Port Kennedy among the pearling luggers in the sluicing
spring tide.

T.I., with its black inhabitants, sandy, wind-blown streets,
tumbledown shacks and thirty pilots who see big ships safely
through the strait and the Great Barrier Reef waters, is a
derelict-looking but entertaining spot. At that time of year,
however, with the south-east monsoon blowing at its strongest,
it is not a restful place for a small vessel, as the anchorage is on
the windward side. So having entered (the usual mass of Australian paper work awaited us at the custom house) and having
bought an anchor—a poor little thing of 28 lb., but all that was
available—we shifted across to the lee of neighbouring Horn
Island, where we lay in great content in smooth water for a day
or two before continuing on our way to Darwin in the Northern
Territory, where mail should lie waiting for us.

10

The Stranding off Croker Island

On leaving Torres Strait we encountered such boisterous weather in the Arafura Sea, which day after day the Australian Broadcasting Commission reported as being 'very rough', that we put in at the well-sheltered bay on the west side of low, uninhabited North Goulburn Island, which lay only 40 miles off our direct course, for a rest. The weather then took a turn for the better, and continued so for the next six weeks with scarcely a cloud, and mostly with light or moderate winds.

Being now close to the coast of Arnhemland, a part of the Northern Territory which is an Aboriginal reserve, wild country not often visited, we thought we might as well take the inshore route to Darwin as being the more interesting thing to do; also we should then be able to find an anchorage each night. But that is something we now have no wish to repeat, for it nearly proved to be our undoing. At that time the area had been only partly surveyed, so that the charts could not be entirely depended on, and the water is so thick and discoloured that the numerous dangers to navigation cannot be seen. The bush-covered coast is flat and featureless, and is penetrated by several shallow rivers inhabited by crocodiles; the only sign of human life is the occasional thin wisp of smoke from a cooking fire, or the heavy pall over an extensive bush fire, for the Aborigine, who has no village life and is usually on 'walkabout', often burns the bush so as to drive out for killing the wild creatures living in it.

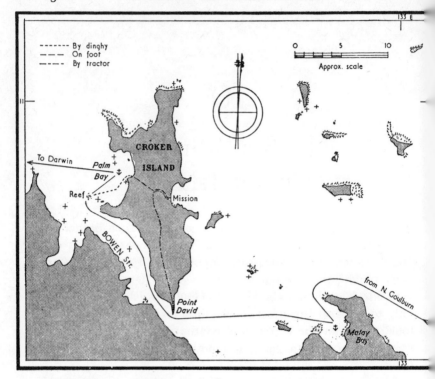

CROKER ISLAND AND APPROACHES

We spent a night at anchor in the dark and silent waters of Malay Bay, and then sailed on to pass through Bowen Strait, which separates Croker Island from the mainland. The strait is 14 miles long and from $1\frac{1}{2}$ to 3 miles wide, and in all its length the chart shows only eight soundings and some mid-channel shoals. Passing Point David, where we could have found good anchorage and so saved ourselves a lot of worry, but it was still too early to think of stopping for the night, we entered the strait and borrowed on the island side to avoid the mid-channel dangers, while Susan kept a look-out from aloft. The green, bush-covered shore of the island slipped quickly past, for the wind was fresh in the strait and *Wanderer* was making good speed in the smooth water. We saw no sign of human life; no canoe lay on the beach, and no thread of smoke showed above the trees; we therefore supposed that the mission shown on the chart, at the island's eastern side, had been abandoned, and that the 180-sq.-mile island was now uninhabited.

The sun was falling low by the time we reached the western end of Bowen Strait, and the obvious anchorage for the night was in Palm Bay on the western side of the island. The chart indicated a shoal running out a distance of 3 miles from the island's western point, and gave a depth of $2\frac{1}{4}$ fathoms over its outer part. To get into the bay before the light failed, we cut across the seaward end of that shoal, where there should have been a depth of $3\frac{1}{4}$ fathoms, for the tide was high and at the top of springs. Susan was still keeping a look-out from the rigging, and when I could leave the helm for a moment I took an occasional sounding. Susan saw nothing, I found no bottom at 5 fathoms, and the ship was sailing fast with the wind abeam and was well heeled when she struck.

We tried to gybe her off, and failed; so we launched the dinghy, laid out an anchor and tried to haul her off, but again failed; she was so hard aground that nothing we could do moved her. Although there was not much swell in the lee of the island, there was sufficient to lift her forepart and drop it again and again on the reef with a sickening crash, so that she shuddered from stem to stern and the mast and rigging vibrated.

An hour after the stranding the wind providentially died away. With some protesting creaks and groans and the occasional furtive shuffle of something moving in a locker, the ship lay over farther and farther as the tide fell, until she was resting deathly still at an angle of 55 deg. At low water the scene from on deck in the light of the full moon shining from the cloudless sky was horrible. All around lay hummocks of coral with pools between in which fish splashed, and it appeared that the ship lay in the centre of an expanse of reef about a quarter of a mile in diameter, and with no apparent way out. The after part of her keel rested on a coral head; her starboard bilge lay low in one of the pools.

Although we had run aground at high-water spring tides, a faint hope of getting off lay in the fact that the predicted tide at Darwin would be a few inches higher in the morning. But the tide at Darwin has a range of 20 ft. and at Croker Island only 6 ft., so any increase in height would be very small. The ship lay so far over that movement about her was difficult; nevertheless we managed to shift all movable weights from aft into the forepeak in an attempt to reduce the draught at the stern, pumped out the freshwater tanks, and relaid the anchor in what appeared to be the least impossible direction for hauling off. Then we tried to get some sleep before the morning tide made, but with little success, for we were anxious, and so acute was the angle of heel that we wondered if the ship would be able to lift with the flood. But of course she did lift, and as the hours dragged slowly by she eased herself degree by degree into a more and more upright position. Then the dreadful pounding began again, for although there was still no wind, the swell was making with the tide. Again the whole ship vibrated with each staggering shock, and it was difficult to keep a foothold, yet she was still hard aground aft. I had lashed the tiller to prevent the rudder from slamming from side to side, but so great was the strain that the tiller—a stout one of English oak— snapped off short in the rudder head. Unable to drive the stump out, we could no longer control the movement of the rudder, and I feared the pintles on which it was hung would be the next to break. Slowly the water crept up, but it stopped rising when still 6 in. short of what was needed to float us. We swung the boom from side to side, jumped together on the foredeck, and hove in on the anchor warp, but without the slightest effect. There seemed to be nothing more that we could do.

'We'll never get her off now,' I said, 'and the evening tide won't rise as high as this.'

'I know.' Susan looked towards the low, moonlit coast of the

PLATE 21

Top: Papuan outrigger canoes, which are said to be among the fastest sailing craft in the world.. *Bottom:* Bramble Cay, at the entrance to the Great North-East Channel, is a speck of land only 10 ft. high for which many navigators have searched for anxious hours. Rarely have we stopped at a place providing such an air of isolation.

island, the nearest point of which lay 3 miles away. We both knew that if the south-east monsoon returned with its usual strength, as it might do at any moment, we would not be able to row our tiny dinghy against it and the short chop of sea it would quickly raise.

'We'd better get ashore while we still can,' I said, but before we abandoned ship we performed such small services as we could for her. In case a tidal wave or other miracle should float her, we dropped the bower anchor and all the chain under foot; we stowed the mainsail, unbent the staysail and squared up the gear on deck. The cabin looked so ordered and civilized in the lamplight, with its green upholstered berths, and polished furniture, its books and pictures, and the small things we had collected on our voyages screwed to the white bulkheads, that I could scarcely believe I was probably looking at it for the last time. I even wound the chronometer.

We put a few irreplaceable belongings—the log-books and visitors' book, the tins of black-and-white negatives and the colour transparencies—into a sail-bag. We also took a spare pair of shoes, tubes of sunburn cream and insect repellent, a Dundee cake in a sealed tin, some chocolate, and a *garafon* of water. We put these things in the stern of the dinghy, and taking an oar each we rowed away in the first pale light of dawn, sadly leaving *Wanderer* there to pound on the reef. As Susan said with tears in her eyes:

'She was such a game little ship.'

Croker Island is 23 miles long on its north and south axis and 10 miles across at its widest. Our hope was that the mission across on the eastern side might still be in operation, or that we might find some Aborigines to look after us, for we would certainly be incapable of looking after ourselves on an island

PLATE 22
Croker Island. *A.* Presently, to our great relief, we came upon a well-beaten double track, which looked as though it had been made by a rubber-tyred vehicle; *B.* and after walking for two hours reached the neat, well-spaced buildings of the mission. *C.* Radio contact was made with the mission ship *Laarpan*, and she came to our assistance. *D.* On the afternoon of our departure the Aborigines of Croker Island staged a corroboree to celebrate *Wanderer*'s escape.

B.W.H.–K

such as this. We did not row to the nearest point, for our intention was to make our way across the island at its narrowest part, thus shortening the journey on foot through the bush.

We rowed for about 5 miles before landing, then dragged the dinghy up the sandy beach and capsized her. By then the sun was well up in the cloudless sky and already the windless day was growing hot. Leaving our valuables under the dinghy and carrying the other things with us, we set out to cross the island, steering as best we could by the sun.

The bush was uncannily silent, but now and then the silence was shattered by the startling screams of white cockatoos. The ground was alive with ants—their giant red-brown anthills stood on every hand—and the air with flies which tormented us. My chief recollection is of a wilderness of gum trees, thousands of them, their silver-grey trunks blocking the view in every direction, though their thin foliage did little to protect us from the sun. We plodded on in single file, sadly and rather silently, our shirts wet with sweat. Neither of us mentioned the matter of snakes, but we both knew that the death adder was to be found on the Arnhemland islands, and our bare legs felt unpleasantly vulnerable. Now and then we sat on a fallen tree for a rest, a drink, and a bite of food, but were quickly driven on again by the attention of the insects. Presently to our great relief we came upon a well-beaten double track which looked as though it had been made by a rubber-tyred vehicle. Although this wound among the trees it led in the general direction we wished to take, so we followed it—the going was very much easier now—and after walking for two hours breasted a slight rise where the bush thinned a bit, and there got a glimpse of the blue sea off the island's eastern side, and were cooled by a breeze. Soon after we came to a large cattle pen and a banana plantation on to which a windmill was pumping water with a cool, rustling noise; and then, to our untold relief, we suddenly reached the neat, wide-spaced buildings of the mission. The first building housed a motor truck, from under which a white man crawled as we approached.

'I don't wish to seem melodramatic,' I said, and somehow my lips did not feel quite steady just then, 'but my wife and I are shipwrecked. We abandoned our boat on a reef off the west coast at dawn.'

He showed no surprise. 'I'm Graham White, the mission carpenter,' he said as he took the bag from Susan's hand and the *garafon* from mine. 'Come along to my home and tell me about it,' and he led the way across the sunburnt grass to his bungalow, where his wife met us and produced some food; but we could not eat.

I asked if there was a motor launch we could borrow, as we would like to salvage some of our personal effects before *Wanderer* broke up.

'Yes, mate,' he replied, 'we've got a launch here, but you won't need it for that. We're going to get your boat off for you.'

'But that's impossible,' said Susan.

'Nothing's impossible if you try hard enough,' was his confident reply, which was echoed by the Mission Superintendent, the Rev. Eric Moore, as soon as he had heard our story.

Those two strong, practical, and self-reliant Australians realized the need for speedy action and good organization if *Wanderer* was to be got afloat before she broke up. By extraordinary good fortune the mission ship *Laarpan*, taking a party of Aboriginal children to Darwin from another mission farther along the coast, was in the vicinity, and would be passing through Bowen Strait that night on her last trip for three months. Radio contact was made with her on the noon schedule, and I spoke with her master, Captain Bill Pringle, who expressed instant willingness to render any help in his power, and mentioned that he had a cargo of empty 44-gallon kerosene drums which might prove useful. A rendezvous was arranged with him for that evening at Point David. Meanwhile the mission launch, which normally is used only for loading and unloading *Laarpan*, was sent off to make the 30-mile trip to the scene of the stranding, a party of Aborigines was rounded up, and food and blankets for the whole expedition were organized, for the mission ship had only enough for her own requirements.

That evening a curious equipage set out from the mission to make its way for 10 miles through the bush to Point David. Eric, looking far from clerical in an old, short-sleeved boiler suit, his handsome face streaked where trickles of sweat darkened the dust with which it was coated, drove the tractor, with Graham perched insecurely on one of the narrow mudguards beside him. Hitched to the drawbar of the tractor was a long, two-wheel, home-made trailer on which squatted the party of Aborigines. Susan and I sat on a pile of blankets among them, our wide-brimmed straw hats pulled down over our eyes, and were almost choked by the fine, black dust stirred up in clouds by the huge, ribbed tyres close in front of us. There was a track of sorts, but it was much overgrown, and often it was necessary to stop while Eric jumped from his seat and with skilled and powerful blows with an axe—he had been a farmer before he took holy orders—felled the young trees or parted the fallen ones which hindered our progress; then on we jolted in a storm of dust to the next hold-up. Our black companions on the trailer regarded the occasion as a great lark, and frequently threw lighted matches, and sometimes whole boxes of matches, into the tinder-like bush; this, no doubt, was a Heaven-sent opportunity for setting fire to a larger than usual area. We could not linger to see what effect these incendiaries had, for it was a race with the oncoming night to make the rendezvous, as it is not possible to drive through country such as this after dark. As it was we only just managed to reach Point David by nightfall.

Laarpan was already lying at anchor there; lights shone from her ports and deckhouse windows, and a buzz of talk came from her party of excited children. A boat was waiting on the beach to take us off to her, and on board we met Bill Pringle. He offered us a shower, for we were unbelievably dusty, and gave us a cup of tea, but otherwise appeared to take no interest in us or in *Wanderer*'s desperate predicament.

As soon as the moon was up we set off through Bowen Strait—much had happened and a long time seemed to have passed since we sailed our own ship through that strait, yet that had been only the previous day. Two Australian school-teachers, who were in charge of the children, had the bunks in Bill's deck cabin, and Susan and I—rolled up in blankets, for although the night was hot we both felt shivery, perhaps due to our physical and mental exhaustion—shared the floor between them. Close beneath us throbbed the Gardner diesel engine, a healthy, heartening sound, for its every revolution was taking us nearer to *Wanderer*. Exhausted, we slept so soundly that we never heard the anchor being let go or the mission launch come alongside. Bill, Eric, and Graham knew that to find *Wanderer* might take some considerable time, for *Laarpan* had not dared to approach the reef at all closely, and it is not easy to see a small white boat on a glassy sea in the moonlight; and they understood that the search would worry us if much prolonged. So they left us sleeping while they went off in the launch to look for her and study the situation at low water, and so as not to wake us they thoughtfully left the main engine running. They never told us this, of course, we had to prise it out of them word by word later. At 2 a.m. the launch returned, and Bill woke us to say that he and his companions had walked all round *Wanderer*, and that apart from a small patch of torn copper sheathing she appeared to be undamaged. We learnt later from Eric that Bill had forgotten to take shoes with him; but that did not deter him, and he made his inspection bare-foot, a very dangerous thing to do because of the risk of stepping on a stonefish; the poison from the sharp spines of these crea-tures, which lie camouflaged and motionless on coral reefs, can cause such unbearable pain that people have died of it. There was also the risk of coral cuts, which can be serious enough, as they often refuse to heal and become septic.

A little before high water the launch again left *Laarpan* with the original party, the two school-teachers, sixteen Aborigines, and ourselves—we wrapped up in blankets, as we were still wearing only the thin shirts and shorts in which we had abandoned ship the previous morning—found her way once more to *Wanderer* and went alongside, Bill giving the strictest orders to fend her off so that the yacht's paintwork should not be marked. At his request Eric said a prayer, which concluded with the simple words:

'God, during the next hour or two we shall be pretty busy and may forget you. Don't you forget us.'

First we trans-shipped all our tinned provisions to the launch and weighed our anchors. How good it was to be back on board *doing* something! Then, when the tide ceased to rise any more, the sixteen Aborigines and the school-teachers came aboard, and with ourselves clustered on the foredeck to weigh the bows down and help lift the stern. Bill stood by the rigging directing operations, while Eric and Graham handled the launch and the line which was now made fast to us. While the twin screws of the launch churned the water, *Wanderer*'s human deck cargo swayed from side to side in unison—a remarkable sight in the cold light of the moon—and this, coupled with their combined weight right forward, freed her stern from the grip of the coral, and she began to move ahead. But there were 200 yds. of reef to cross, and again and again she struck, and for agonizing moments hung there rolling, before being dragged off to strike the next lump. The water round her was clouded with the coral she pulverized as the swell smashed her down on it. But at last she was free. We anchored her in deep water and took aboard our stores and restowed them, while our helpers returned to their ship to have breakfast and await full daylight. Then *Laarpan* came, took our line and towed us gently to a safe anchorage in Palm Bay, where she lay alongside while she filled our tanks with fresh water from her own. The sun shone, we were surrounded by friends, our hearts were light, and it was a most memorable occasion. All the children came aboard to have a look at our ship; they filed down the companionway, looked about the cabin with wide, bright eyes, and climbed out by way of the forehatch. Obviously they had never seen anything quite like this before, but the item which most intrigued them was our little w.c. in the forepeak; Bill stood beside it and solemnly demonstrated the working of its chrome-plated pumps to their delighted amazement.

To our great relief we found that stout little *Wanderer* was making no water, and we blessed William King's good shipwrights at Burnham-on-Crouch who had put such excellent workmanship and fine materials into her. Apart from the broken tiller, which Graham neatly repaired, there was no visible damage; but of course, there might well be trouble below the waterline, for it had been possible to examine only one side of the bottom while the ship lay on her side on the reef, and she had since taken some hard blows while being towed to deep water. However, as sharks and crocodiles are known to frequent Palm Bay—an outcrop of flat rock on the beach close to where we landed in the dinghy is said to be a favourite basking place for the latter, which Eric told me can move as fast as a man can run—naturally nobody cared to dive down to take a look.

In a very different frame of mind from that of our last visit, we spent a night at the mission, where we gave a slide show. The mission is one of five in Arnhemland run by the Methodist Church, and its particular job is the care and preparation for adult life on the mainland of up to fifty neglected part-Aboriginal children, ranging from infants to 18-year-olds. They are looked after in cottage units each housing up to ten children, and are there brought up as part of the family by white Australian 'sisters'. It seemed to us a wonderfully happy and healthy community, and we formed the highest opinion of the band of able and enthusiastic people who have dedicated their lives to that work. Although our stranding had been the worst experience of our sailing lives, it is one we are now glad to have had, because it has given us a peep into the lives of those people and shown us how, in an emergency, strangers will come to one's assistance willingly and efficiently without a thought of their own safety or convenience, personal gain or prestige. Their wants were simple, and their only immediate need was a high-quality tape-recorder on which to record and play back Bible stories and singing in the local language. This they now possess, but we owe them a debt of gratitude we can never properly repay.

On the afternoon of our departure the Aborigines of the island staged a corroboree to celebrate *Wanderer*'s escape. With bodies, heads, and faces plastered with blue clay on which crude designs had been daubed, and with long spears in their hands, they gave such a ferocious display of warlike dancing and prancing to the monotonous two-tone throb of the *didgeridoo* (a 4–5 ft. length of hollowed-out wood, balanced on the big toe and blown into) that we felt glad our visit was in 1961 and not one hundred years earlier.

The wind was light and the sea quiet throughout our 160-mile trip to Darwin. There Captain Noble, the harbourmaster, introduced us to the right people and *Wanderer* was quickly hauled out of the water free of charge. The only damage we could find after those four tides spent on the reef was a bent stem-band, some dents in the lead keel and deadwood, and the few square inches of stripped copper sheathing which Bill had noticed.

11

Indian Ocean Crossing

The Top End, as the people who live in Darwin call their part of Australia, was in the news while we were there; plans were afoot for the capture with tranquillizing darts of some indigenous cattle, at a place with the improbable name of Humpty Doo, in the hope of domesticating them and producing beef; mining also was going ahead. The town, which is the capital of the Northern Territory, and is served by one road only, known as 'the track', is not now the wild-west place it used to be, and many long-distance aircraft call there. The buildings are modern, there are several chrome-plated milk-bars in the 'better end' of Smith Street, it has a broadcasting station and a Navy base. We found its people friendly and helpful, but we were unable to stay much longer than our slipping and repairs took, and in one respect that was just as well: the harbour is no place for a small yacht when the south-east monsoon is blowing fresh, for it is exposed to a long drift.

From Darwin west for 1,400 miles to Christmas Island we had almost perfect sailing; indeed, we had nearly forgotten that an ocean passage could be so enjoyable. For the first three days the wind was light, but as there was no swell we did not suffer from the slamming of sails which is the usual accompaniment to such conditions. Until then *Wanderer*'s best day's run had been 157 sea miles; but during this passage she achieved runs on three consecutive days of 166, 169, and 164 miles, and she made good a distance of 1,032 miles in a week. That was *real* sailing, and emphasized how efficient a vehicle a small sailing craft can be when given the right conditions. Sometimes she ran self-steering under the twin rig, giving us a rest from the helm; but most of the time the wind was too far out on the quarter, and the rig was mainsail and one of the twins; then, of course, we had to steer, but although the sky was cloudless the days were never too hot.

With a depth of 150 fathoms only 3 cables offshore, Christmas Island offers no anchorage to large craft or small, so we berthed with our bows to a buoy close inshore and a stern line to the new jetty, which was built for the purpose of handling the motor barges whose job it is to moor between enormous buoys the ships which call to load phosphate. The barges, ten of them, lie in a great boathouse ashore. When one is needed a transporter crane lifts it on to a low truck on rails. A tractor tows the truck out to the end of the jetty, where another crane lifts the barge and swings it out over the water. The crew go aboard, the engine is started, and the barge is then lowered into the water, where the release gear is quickly slipped. The reason for this elaborate and costly arrangement is that sometimes a heavy swell rolls into the cove; then it is unsafe for vessels to lie afloat there. The crewmen of the barges, many of whom come from Keeling Cocos, an atoll lying 530 miles to the west, display great skill when handling their craft and the quarter-mile lengths of heavy steel cable used for mooring ships all-fours.

We lay at Christmas Island for three days, provisioning (that can be done well and cheaply there), seeing the improvements that have been made in recent years to the methods of mining and loading phosphate, and enjoying the wonderful hospitality of the people. But our berth was an uneasy one, open as it was to the ocean, with the constant restless sound of waves breaking on the near-by beach and sucking at the cliffs, and all the time in one's mind was the thought that it might be necessary to put to sea at a few minutes' notice should the swell build up beyond its normal height. So it was with feelings of some relief that we slipped our moorings and sailed on in fine weather for Keeling Cocos, carrying with us letters and parcels from the Christmas Island Cocos-Malays to their relatives on Cocos, for although the islands are so near to one another there is virtually no communication between them. Everyone offered us 'postage' in the form of cowry and cat's-eye shells.

Our landfall was a line of green palm tops nodding above the uneven horizon as we lifted on the swell. That morning the wind was strong, the sea was rough, and a procession of rain squalls marched down upon us as we ran fast towards the atoll under the close-reefed mainsail only. Often several feet of the boom plunged shudderingly into the sea, and at those moments the ship pulled hard on the helm. With the sea breaking heavily on the coral close to leeward, I felt that this was not the time or place for anything to go wrong, and I wondered about the tiller, which Graham White had repaired at Croker Island, for he had expressed some doubts about its strength, and advised me to get a new one as soon as possible; but that was something I had failed to obtain at Darwin, because there was no suitable piece of timber there. However, all went well and we were soon in the shelter of the sparkling lagoon, where the turquoise colouring of the water was of breath-taking beauty. We worked our way to windward among the reefs and came to a perfect anchorage in 3 fathoms of crystal-clear water a few yards from the smooth sandy beach on the lee side of Direction Island. There we lay in quiet water so sheltered by the palms that only a gentle breeze reached us, while over at the other side of our thin, crescent-shaped island the sea thundered with a loud, continuous roar, giving us a pleasant feeling of snug security.

The island is shared by the cable-relay station and the marine base, which mans and maintains the landing barges and rescue launches used in connexion with the air strip over on West Island. We were immediately engulfed by lavish, offhand Australian hospitality, and towards the end of our stay we tried to repay a little of this by giving a slide show and talk followed by a beer-drinking party at our expense in the cable-station club, to which everyone on the island, except the watch-keeper and some children, came—about twenty-five all told. The surroundings were the most glamorous in which we have ever performed; the screen was placed out in the open in front of the club veranda, and the lagoon, the palms, and the star-filled sky made the backdrop. The party, at which an astonishing quantity of beer was drunk, continued until the not so early hours of the next morning, and when we tried to settle up with the Mess President he refused to let us pay for more than a little of it. The cable station depends on rain for its water supply. But there had been no rain for some time, and as each of the six houses for married men is provided with a washing machine, there was naturally a grave shortage and everyone was being rationed; so we did not like to take the small quantity needed to top up our tanks. However, the marine base was better off, for it has a solar still, so we got our needs there.

In the absence abroad of John Clunies Ross, who owns the Keeling Cocos Islands, his cousin Gerry was managing Home Island, and on several occasions he came over in a motor launch to collect us and carry us back at terrifying speed over the lagoon coral—on which it seemed the boat's bottom must surely be ripped open—to have curry lunch with him and his wife Lettie in their cool Home Island house. Four hundred Cocos-Malays live on that island, and theirs appeared to be a happy, contented, and healthy community under the benevolent rule of the Clunies Ross family. There are no disturbing influences from the outside world, for there is hardly any contact with it except the occasional supply ship, and Australians from the other islands of the atoll may only visit there by special invitation.

The economy is based entirely on the coconut. Each weekday morning, and usually before dawn, the men of the island set out in their *jugongs* to gather coconuts from the other islands bordering the lagoon. Each man to earn his pay must gather 500 nuts a day, husk them, load them into his *jugong*, and sail them back to Home Island. There the women take over, splitting the nuts open, removing the meat, and putting it in the driers, which are fired by the husks; the final drying is done on racks in the sun. Everyone gets a basic ration of rice and bread, and there is plenty of fish, and sometimes turtle, to be

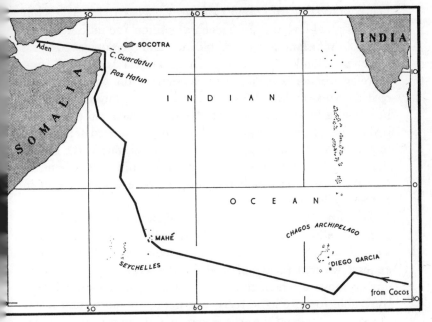

WESTERN PART OF INDIAN OCEAN

had in the lagoon. The *jugong* incidentally is a carvel-built, double-ended open boat, often with hard chines; it is fast and very crank. All have been built on the island, and each man has his own. They are gunter-rigged and, strangely enough, are steered with a yoke and lines.

Gerry kindly gave *Wanderer* a present of a new tiller which he had one of his skilled shipwrights make from a beautiful piece of satin-smooth *bungnwar*, which had come from Christmas Island in the days when there was occasional steamer connexion with that island.

Soon after we had left Cocos the Indian Ocean, which so far had been kind to us, began to show its true character; the wind became strong, the sea got up, and there was much rain, enough even to slake the thirst of the washing machines at Cocos; also, contrary to expectations, we had a current against instead of with us.

On our way to the Seychelles we had hoped to stop at

Diego Garcia, southernmost of the Chagos Archipelago, but when we had by account reached a position 120 miles to windward of that island a gale was blowing and the sky was overcast with rain clouds. Like Cocos, Diego Garcia is an atoll, and therefore cannot be seen until it is near. To the north and west of it lie banks on which the sea is said to heap up dangerously in bad weather. As we did not care to approach closer without being sure of our position, we hove-to and waited for the sky to clear. And so we remained for three days, but at the end of that time the weather still showed no sign of improvement, so we left the atoll to its wind and rain, and bore away for Mahé in the Seychelles Group.

To set out on a 1,400-mile trip and suddenly find it lengthened by an additional 1,000 miles is bad for the morale; but as we had not relied on obtaining any provisions at Diego Garcia, at least we had plenty of food for this unpleasant extension, during most of which the weather was bad. Occasionally we were able to unroll the reefs, but never for more than a few hours at a time, and the greater part of the trip was made under the close-reefed mainsail or the trysail, though sometimes we were able to set one of the spinnakers as well. Often the sky was smeary, there were solar and lunar haloes and frequent downpours of rain.

The Seychelles, ninety-two islands belonging to Britain, are set on a huge shallow bank, and we made a point of crossing the perimeter of that bank in a place where the soundings are not less than 12 fathoms, because we thought that the heavy sea then running might heap up or break on shoaler spots. Having done that, we altered course for Port Victoria on Mahé, the largest and most important of the islands. After a wild night of wind and rain, we sighted the mist-capped mountains at dawn of our twenty-sixth day out from Cocos, and in the forenoon rounded a group of protecting islands and came into smooth water. Then with almost bewildering suddenness, for the place is small and we were sailing fast, we found ourselves in the inner harbour, where we rounded up off Long Pier (truly named, for it is half a mile in length) and anchored. As soon as we had been

granted pratique, Harvey Brain, who owned a 40-ft. motor
fishing vessel and proved to be an entertaining and kindly
companion, came off and piloted us through an awkward
little channel to a sheltered berth alongside his own ship at
Short Pier.

Mahé, only 15 miles long and 5 miles wide at its narrowest,
is a remarkably beautiful island; its mountains rise to 3,000 ft.
and are encircled by a narrow coastal plain where palms over-
hang the empty beaches. The only town is Victoria, mostly a
picturesque huddle of timber buildings with red iron roofs,
and such native villages as we saw were of thatch and well
shaded by trees. We found the Creoles courteous but lacking
the friendliness and spontaneous gaiety which is the delightful
heritage of the inhabitants of so many of the small islands at
which we have called. Mahé is poverty-stricken, but plans were
afoot for a fishing industry, and it was hoped to encourage
tourists to go there. Such an attractive place should prove
popular, and the cost of living, even in the hotels, struck us as
being absurdly cheap; but as it is so far from anywhere (1,000
miles from Mombasa and 1,700 miles from Bombay) and has no
air communication one wonders where the tourists are to come
from.

We could have enjoyed a much longer stay than the eight
days we allowed ourselves, but the north-west monsoon, with
its accompanying bad weather, was likely to set in soon, and we
knew from the pilot charts that if we did not manage to get
round Cape Guardafui (the north-east corner of Africa) by the
end of October, we would most probably encounter a strong
headwind and contrary current.

Our last night in the island we spent in North West Bay off
Beau Vallon, for Gerry le Grand had invited us to dine at his
hotel, which lies beneath the palms on the shore there in as
glamorous a setting as one could imagine. Landing at dusk was
exciting, for a considerable swell was running in from the open
ocean, and no small dinghy makes a good surf-boat. However,
Gerry with some of his guests waded out into the surf and
shouted instructions, telling us when to pull and when to back,

and as we came surging in on the back of a breaker, they grabbed our dinghy and carried her quickly up the beach before the next breaker arrived.

We spent a most pleasant evening at the hotel, where first we had iced drinks at the Goggle and Flipper, the beachside bar, and then dined to the accompanying rustle of palms and boom of surf. I was sitting next to Gerry's wife, and thinking what a pleasant and easygoing place this must be, I asked her how long she had lived there.

'Nine years,' she replied wearily, 'and I've hated every moment of it.' But she then went on to explain that she had a young family at school in Kenya, and because there was no air service she was able to see the children only rarely.

The business of getting back to *Wanderer*, whose riding light gleamed a bright pinpoint far out in the bay, proved to be even more exciting than the arrival had been, for our friends could help us only a little way into the surf. But, as before, they shouted instructions and encouragement, and although both oars jumped out of the rowlocks as we were mounting a particularly steep breaker, we re-shipped them quickly and managed to get away safely. Next morning, after Gerry had come off with a gift of fruit and fresh-baked bread, we left for Aden 1,400 miles away to the north and west.

It was a little late in the season to be setting out on that trip, and we could expect only light winds. But at least they should be fair as far as the Equator (unless the north-west monsoon broke in the meantime) and from any direction thereafter until we reached Cape Guardafui; we could expect 12 per cent of calm and no gales. And so it proved to be, except that the winds were even lighter than the pilot chart indicated. We took two days to get clear of the Seychelles Bank, and another three to reach the Equator, and in the first week at sea managed to make good only 355 miles. The second week was even worse, with only 281 miles to the good, and for part of the time we

PLATE 23
The economy of Keeling Cocos depends on the coconut. Each man gathers 500 nuts a day; the women split them open and remove and dry the meat.

were becalmed, achieving once a day's run of 0, the two consecutive noon positions on the chart being right on top of one
another. After that we grew a little anxious, for we fell in with a
west-setting current with a rate of about 1 knot, and this carried
us steadily towards the African coast. Somewhere near the coast
(the position varies from month to month and is not clearly
indicated on the pilot charts) the current splits, one part
running north-north-east towards Guardafui, the other part
running south-west towards Zanzibar. If we made the coast
north of the dividing line, all would be well and we would
receive a fine push on our way; but should we make our landfall too far south, and at that time we had little say in the
matter, we might find it necessary to struggle back to Seychelles, re-provision there, and try again.

Apart from the fact that there was no sea and very little
swell, the conditions were trying. The sea temperature was
80°F., and in the middle of the day the cabin temperature was
well up in the nineties. The atmosphere was humid, and when
there was no air stirring our overheated bodies could not re-
frigerate in the normal way, and we sat damply in puddles of
our own making, waiting for the slight relief the hours of darkness would bring. The sky at dawn was magnificent; nearly
every day a colourful display was put on for our benefit, or so
it seemed, for there was nobody else around to enjoy it except
a few seabirds, some Portuguese men-of-war, and jumping
sting-rays, the latter making a noise like gunfire when they
landed with a crash on their bellies. Sometimes the evening sky
was cloudless, and we then watched the unwinking disk of the
sun become distorted to a pear shape and plunge below the
horizon, and we looked for the green flash; once Susan, by
rising to her feet and thus increasing her height of eye as the
flash occurred, prolonged the moment appreciably.

Daybreak of our eighteenth day at sea showed the faint outline of the African coast, the coast of Somalia, and cloud having

PLATE 24
Soon after we had left Keeling Cocos the Indian Ocean showed its true character,
and for many days we ran fast with strong winds and rough seas.

B.W.H.–L

prevented star sights, we looked forward eagerly to noon, when we should learn what the current had been doing with us. The sun shone clearly, but when I had worked out our noon position I could scarcely believe my observations, for they put us 68 miles ahead of the dead reckoning position. However, further observations in the afternoon and evening confirmed them, so with great relief we knew we were in the north-going stream— and what a stream that was, with a rate of nearly 3 knots. Guardafui now lay only 200 miles ahead, but we took another four days to reach it, for such little wind as there was came from ahead, and after we had passed the peninsula of Ras Hafum we were again becalmed, and just where we expected to find the current running at its hardest we found no current at all; yet we were among what appeared to be strong tide-rips and overfalls, but these may have been due to an upwelling of cold water.

The waters off this corner of Africa, particularly south of Socotra, can certainly be difficult for small craft. About this area the *Pilot* remarks that currents of between 4 and 5½ knots have often been reported, and there have been occasional reports of 6 knots and over, which are greater than are known in any other oceanic region. This area is also reported to have, in July, a higher percentage frequency of gales than any other part of the open ocean, within the tropics: 20 per cent of force 8 and over. Off Cape Horn the highest figure is 30 per cent.

The arid coast with its 3,000-ft. mountains is spectacular, and although in itself Cape Guardafui is not particularly impressive, it was looking quite lovely when we rounded it at dawn, for its grey cliffs were gold- and pink-washed by the first low rays of the sun. Just beyond the headland we came upon a large village, its huts squatting on the sloping sand of the desert, which here comes rolling down to the sea. We saw no blade of grass or other vegetation, yet there were many people about and herds of goats. We wondered what they lived on, and felt tempted to stop and investigate, but the light breeze was onshore, and the anchorage a poor one. Later, at Aden, we were told it was probably just as well we did not stop, as the people in that part of Somalia have the reputation of being unfriendly and might have robbed us. At first hearing such suggestions are hard to take seriously, but now and then an incident proves their truth. For example, a few years before an American single-handed sailor by the name of Peterson had the misfortune to strand on a reef near Mocha in the Yemen, little more than a hundred miles from Aden. He was thrown into prison for some days and was released only to find that his ship had been looted. More recently, indeed only a short time before we arrived at Aden, a German put in at a small port in the Protectorate; his ship also was looted and he was badly beaten up. We carry a 12-bore shotgun as a defence weapon, but certainly would be sorry to find ourselves in a situation where it was needed for that purpose.

In the Gulf of Aden we expected to find the north-east monsoon established, but calms and light airs persisted, and not until we neared Aden did we pick up a decent breeze. That gave us a run of 150 miles, and during the afternoon of our twenty-fifth day at sea the sharp peaks of the Aden Peninsula stood starkly against the pale blue sky ahead. We did not attempt to enter the harbour that night, but worked our way in to a quiet anchorage under the lee of the outer breakwater—and slept.

Normally we do not make use of letters of introduction, for we feel that they place an unfair obligation on their recipients, and we prefer to make our friends in a less formal way. But a large commercial port, such as Aden, can be awkward for a visiting yacht, and as we wished to remain some time and refit there, I had written in advance to Major-General Bray, a fellow member of the Royal Cruising Club, who was then stationed there. He had to return to England before we arrived, but he left in train arrangements for us to be well looked after. One result of this was that when we went into the harbour next morning and landed we were met on the beach near Post Office Pier by a uniformed reception committee consisting of Colonel Pallot, Commander of the Garrison, and

Commander Alan-Williams, Resident Naval Officer; both are sailing men, and they came with offers of hospitality and assistance. The former had all our long-awaited mail, a car to take us to the bank and shops, a Sultan's bathroom, which he placed at our disposal, and an invitation from his wife to dinner on that and other nights. The Commander at once organized a safe and comfortable berth for *Wanderer* at the Navy pier, the best berth in the whole harbour, where a neighbouring mothballed minesweeper sheltered her from the prevailing north-easter and the floating oil, and he and his wife were also most hospitable.

PLATE 25
Sometimes the evening sky was almost cloudless, and then we watched the unwinking disk of the sun plunge below the horizon.

12

The Red Sea and Suez Canal

We remained at Aden for all of November and half of December, and that was not a day too long, for we found our first visit to the Middle East both interesting and enjoyable in spite of the heat, the dust, the flies, the stink, and the importunate shopkeepers who seemed able to strip the cash from the passengers of a large ship in a few hours—cameras, radio sets, tape-recorders and typewriters all being duty-free—and as 500 ships a month put into the port for bunkers, the supply of passengers was unending. Hospitality was at times almost overwhelming, and we were particularly grateful to Derek Import, a B.B.C. engineer and Port Officer for the Little Ship Club, who took us by Land Rover to get a glimpse of the Protectorate. The only road out of Aden is the beach, firm sand washed twice a day by the tide, and smooth going with a driver like Derek, who knows how to avoid the soft patches; on one side the Indian Ocean swell broke in long ranks of wind-driven foam, and on the other the desert stretched to the horizon. We drove along it for 40 miles, and then lurched inland to the town of Ga'ar, where the English District Adviser always has an armed bodyguard of two soldiers, and the fort might have been lifted straight out of one of P. C. Wren's novels; hostages from dissident tribes are held there in a generally successful effort to preserve the peace. Cotton grows

PLATE 26
Top: Only a few miles from this squalid Arab fishing village is the port of Aden, where 500 ships a month put in for bunkers; *bottom,* and the place is as busy by night as it is by day.

near the town, but much of the country is desert, mile upon mile of rock, stone, and undulating sand across which the swaying camel trains make their way. Everyone goes armed and there are few women to be seen. On other expeditions we visited the teeming town of Sheik'Othman, and Fuqum fishing village, where houses made from packing-cases and oil drums sprawl on the beach, and the word *baksheesh* echoes on every side, while the goats chew the fishing nets and the sun beats down from a cloudless sky. Within a mile or so of that squalid little place lie in neat rows the air-conditioned homes of the staff of the B.P. oil refinery at Little Aden; there the tankers discharge and the oil is refined and pumped across to feed the ships at Aden.

Charts present something of a problem for a small yacht on a long voyage. With the exception of the American set for the Galápagos Islands, we used British Admiralty charts exclusively, and for the whole circumnavigation we needed about 800. Although we can carry 400 we do not find it convenient to have more than about 250 on board, so we arranged for J. D. Potter, the London chart agent, to send sets of charts out to meet us at certain ports, and then sent home those we had finished with. This had the additional advantage that the charts we were about to use were up to date. At Aden we shipped all that we should need to get us as far as Rhodes. It is always an exciting business undoing a roll of crisp, new charts, which try to behave like clock springs, but smell pleasantly of printer's ink and good paper, arranging them in geographical order (I do not know what method Potter uses when packing, but certainly it is not geographical or numerical), and making a preliminary study of them and the *Pilot*, reading and trying to pronounce for the first time a string of strange names, and taking a particularly careful look at any harbour plans to find out what sort of anchorages lie ahead and how easy or difficult they are of access. The charts we took aboard at Aden were a more exciting bunch than usual, for they covered, among other things, the whole of the Red Sea and Gulf of Suez. These were waters which, whenever we had thought or spoken of them, had sent apprehensive tickles down our spines. But always they had lain far distant, and we had not worried about them overmuch, preferring to concentrate on the more immediate problems of the passage in hand or about to be undertaken. But now we were on the threshold of the Red Sea, and the hazards associated with it in our minds loomed large, and now would have to be grappled with at last.

Much of our time and energy at Aden was taken up with *Wanderer*'s refit. To paint the sides we needed quieter water than was to be found at the Navy pier, and the R.A.F. kindly gave us permission to lie at its marine base at the eastern end of the harbour. There we had the pleasure of meeting two other cruising couples: Tom and Janet Steele (American) in the Tahiti ketch *Adios*, and Blue and Dot Bradfield (Australian) in *D'Vara*, a boat they had built with their own hands to one of the late Harrison Butler's designs, and rigged as a wishbone ketch. Tom had already made one circumnavigation of the globe in *Adios*. After that he married, and now with his beautiful blonde Janet was making a second round trip complete with washing machine and motor cycle. I doubt if ever before two small yachts, both with world voyages to their credit, have met during their second circumnavigations, and this certainly was a great occasion for us.

Like ourselves, both couples were bound north up the Red Sea, and, of course, we all spent a lot of time discussing the prospects. I said that because of the strong headwind in the northern half, the reefs which run out from both shores, the not always friendly people, and the mass of shipping in the middle, I thought this likely to be the most difficult and possibly the most dangerous part of the whole trip.

'Sure, sure,' Tom agreed, 'it's a mean bit of water. Janet and I plan to keep out in the middle and motor like hell when we can.'

But Blue thought that Tom and I were making altogether too much fuss about it.

'We'll work the inshore passages,' he drawled. 'There are plenty of anchorages, and Dot wants to do a bit of fossicking, as she's found a market for her shells.'

Somehow it was a comfort to know that these yachts were going our way, even though we were unlikely to see much, if anything, of them—we had been on our own for such a long time—but both had motors of greater power than *Wanderer*'s, and fuel for a considerable distance, enough, I believe, to motor the whole way, if necessary.

A short row from the R.A.F. base was the small ship harbour where dhows from Zanzibar, Somalia, and the Persian Gulf came to discharge, refit, and load. Characterful and strikingly beautiful craft we thought them, with their high decorated poops, hanging privys, and lateen rig. But there was little movement under sail in the harbour, because most of them are now fitted with auxiliary engines.

On leaving Aden we had a jolly little sail for 20 miles along the coast to a pleasant anchorage off the fishing village which lies inside Ras Imran. The usual huddle of jerry-built huts cowered on the sand at the foot of an impressive black cliff 700 ft. high, the only access to it being along the beach, at the far end of which stood a cluster of jeeps by means of which the fish are taken to market at Aden. Then on again we went for a day and a night, meeting several dhows under sail, to Perim Island, which lies in the Straits of Bab-el-Mandeb, the southern gateway to the Red Sea, where we remained for some days, as I had an attack of blood poisoning and needed to take a course of penicillin—not the best preparation for the difficulties which lay ahead. Once Perim was a busy coaling station, but it has long since fallen on lean days. The quays and buildings are in ruins, and fishing is the only industry, but the friendly islanders told us that as they have no sufficiently fast and seaworthy boats to make the trip to Aden, the only way of getting their catch to market is to land it on the mainland and take it by jeep along the beach. However, the corrupt police now demand such high bribes to let the jeeps go through that the business is not economic.

A fresh south-easter was blowing when we left Perim. That is the prevailing wind in the southern half of the Red Sea at that time of year, and is one of the reasons why December to

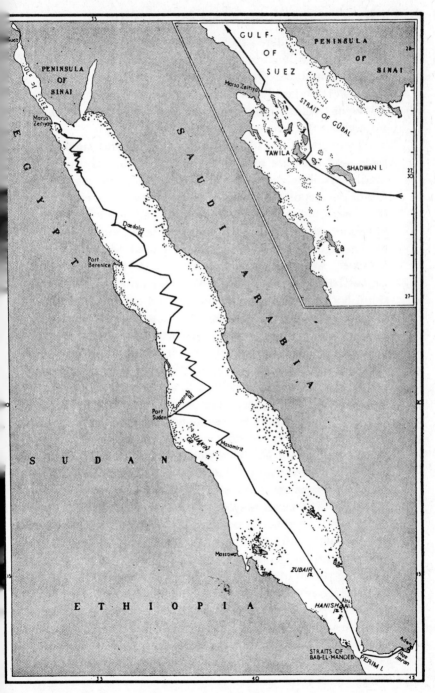

THE RED SEA WITH INSET OF THE STRAIT OF GŪBAL

February is considered the least unsuitable time of year for a north-bound sailing vessel to attempt the Red Sea passage. We could reasonably expect that wind to carry us to, or nearly as far as, Port Sudan, but after that we would have to face strong headwinds which, interspersed with occasional calms, prevail throughout the year in the northern half.

As we left the island astern our fair wind increased to gale force, and we were soon running fast on our way under the small staysail only. It was a wild day and a wild night, by no means the sort of weather to go looking for an anchorage among the coral-fringed Hanish Islands, as had been our original intention; so we hurried on, leaving those islands to port, and in the early hours of the morning passed through Abu Ali Channel, and then altered course a little to go west of the Zubair Islands 70 miles ahead. We shared the night with many ships, both north- and south-bound, and our small staysail rig had the advantage that gybing, which was many times necessary to keep clear of the ships, presented no problem and could be done without disturbing the watch below. None of the ships caused us any serious anxiety; each kept steadily on her course, and whenever we saw masthead lights in line we immediately took avoiding action, because we know quite well that our own low-power navigation lamps cannot be seen for any great distance. However, we do deplore the modern tendency to place ships' masthead lights close together, for the closer together they are the longer does a change of course take to open them, and some ships move so fast that a comparatively slow-moving sailing vessel may need to take action before the red and green sidelights can be seen. If the present trend in naval architecture continues, ships will soon have no masts from which to display lights; and already some new liners have only one little stump of a mast, and no proper position in which to fly flags. To my eye the hulls of these modern vessels are sweet, purposeful, and very lovely, but the upperworks appear to have been designed, like washing machines and refrigerators, to travel at 100 miles an hour, by second-grade art students.

Our first day out from Perim we ran 128 miles, and for

most of the time we were under the small staysail alone; then the wind moderated, and by the following night we were under full sail. After passing the Zubair Islands our course slowly drew away to the west of the main shipping lane, for we were heading towards Masamarit light, which marks the north-eastern corner of the extensive Suakin group of reefs and islets, which we had to round to reach Port Sudan.

The Red Sea is about 1,000 miles in length, and coral reefs lie off both shores. These are usually in patches, but sometimes in big blocks of 100 miles or so; in places they stretch seaward for 50 miles, and except in the approaches to Massawa and Port Sudan are not lighted or marked. In some areas there are channels near the shore inside the reefs; these are sometimes used by small craft with local knowledge, but pilotage in them has to be done by eye, and an anchorage must be found before nightfall. Tom and Ann Worth, able and efficient circumnavigators in *Beyond*, attempted the inshore channel on leaving Port Sudan, but found it was not worth the anxious watching and pilotage, and they had a disturbing incident when sharing an anchorage with a dhow. We therefore planned to stay out in the middle, but there one has many ships to avoid, for an average of 1,000 a month pass through. Clearly the Red Sea is not an easy or pleasant place for a small sailing vessel.

Christmas Eve found us becalmed, so unashamedly we motored, for at Aden we had taken aboard an extra 24 gallons of petrol in jerry-cans for use on occasions such as this, thereby increasing our range under power from 80 to about 200 miles. We would have done well to eat our Christmas dinner and drink the bottle of champagne friends at Aden had given us then and there, for Christmas Day came in rough with a fresh headwind, and well reefed down and plunging into the steep head-sea with spray flying, we had little appetite. But at least we were able to lay Masamarit light close-hauled on the starboard tack.

That afternoon we lost the patent log rotator. This was an old friend which in our 4-ton *Wanderer II* we had towed for many thousands of miles. In *Wanderer III* we had towed the same rotator round the world, and now, after it had spun merrily on the present trip for 25,000 miles, it was, presumably, taken by some large fish which had nothing better for its Christmas dinner.

By midnight we were up with the feeble little Masamarit light, but could not safely weather it; indeed, the wind backed a point or two then, so that even if we could have scraped round we would not have cleared the northern side of the Suakin Group. So we had to put about, and for the next day and a half we plugged to windward against a strong wind and a steep sea, endeavouring to make a sufficient offing from the reefs so that we could fetch in on a westerly course towards Port Sudan.

Navigationally this period became something of a nightmare. Even though we hove-to for our sights, they were difficult enough to take because of the rough sea, and sometimes they placed us as many as 15 miles from where we thought we were. Possibly this was due to currents, which in the Red Sea can run strongly in any direction, but more likely to refraction, a common navigational hazard in those waters, where the false horizon can cause an error of 10 miles in latitude and 20 miles in longitude. When possible we checked our latitude with observations of Polaris, which are easy to take, as that star can be found by setting the sextant to one's approximate latitude and sweeping the northern horizon with the instrument; but the conditions were too rough to permit other star sights to be taken, in which the star must be brought to the horizon, or the horizon to the star.

This, I thought, was just where the new instrument we had shipped at Aden, a radio direction-finding set, could help, for Port Sudan has an air radio beacon of which we could take bearings, and when we had reached its latitude it would be safe to steer for Port Sudan. But the bearings did not make sense, for they put us way down among the Suakin Group, and obviously we were not there. At the time I blamed this on my own lack of skill, but I learnt later from the master of a British

PLATE 27
Northward bound through the Suez Canal, we soon got used to meeting large ships at close quarters.

freighter also bound for Port Sudan from the south that his D/F set had produced the same result as ours. So presumably the position of the beacon had been changed, but the Sudanese had not bothered to tell anyone, as there was no mention of the change in the latest corrections to the *List of Radio Signals*.

However, in time we reached a position from which I considered it was safe to steer direct for the powerful Sanganeb light outside Port Sudan. Shortly after supper on 27 December we sighted the loom of the light in the misty atmosphere, and with the utmost relief, for by then a strong gale was blowing, and we were reaching under the close-reefed mainsail only in what I regarded as a dangerous sea. In the early hours of the morning we had the light abeam, and hove-to for the rest of the night in the comparatively quiet water in the lee of the reef on which it stands, and sailed into the port after breakfast. Half the Red Sea, but the easiest half, was now astern.

The small harbour is a busy one, for it is the only outlet for the entire country, and there was a constant coming and going of ships of many nationalities; some of them remained for many days, as the single-line railway to Khartoum and the antiquated methods of handling cargo—much of it done by gangs of wild-looking Fuzzy-wuzzies with mops of filthy, matted hair—constituted a bottleneck. We found the police too much in evidence. They stopped us taking photographs in the town, and always there was one on the little jetty at which we landed to examine our shopping bags; he even tried to prevent us from taking aboard the stores for which we had paid a high price ashore. But Susan soon fixed that, for she has discovered that if she tells a policeman firmly but with a smile what he is to do, he usually does it without question—I doubt if this would work in London. Apart from two pleasant young men at the Eastern Telegraph Company office, who kindly had us to dine in their mess and enabled us to see something of the desert hinterland

PLATE 28
Our hosts at Cairo gave us their skyscraper bedroom. *Top:* From one of its windows we could look down upon the Nile close beneath, where feluccas sailed; *bottom,* and from the other out over the roof-tops of the city, sharp cubes of brown and yellow.

and the foothills, we made no friends among the seventy British residents. But we did meet Dr. Grant, a young American who, while sailing single-handed down the Red Sea a few days before, had the misfortune to strike a reef; his yacht *Picotee* drove ashore to become a total loss just north of the Sudan/ Egypt border.

We left with few regrets on 9 January 1962. The wind was dead ahead and strong, and we started the long, hard struggle to make northing, a struggle which, apart from occasional short calm intervals totalling 33 hours, when we motored, was to continue for the next fourteen days. Except when under power, *Wanderer*, with the tiller free and usually under the double-reefed mainsail and small staysail, steered herself all the time. We were heartened by the progress she made in those severe conditions. Smashing into the steep head-sea, she flung spray all over herself and up as high as the lower crosstrees; the sun dried the brown terylene sails almost at once, so that their lower parts were often white with salt. And all the time she drove ahead, sailing each day something between 40 and 90 miles through the water, and making good between 20 and 45 miles of northing. Never once during that 540-mile stretch of windward work did the wind permit us to lay the direct course; always it moderated a little in the forenoon and blew hardest at night, and on seven occasions, all during the hours of darkness, we found it necessary to heave-to and wait for conditions to improve. Apart from the strong wind, the weather was lovely; the sky was cloudless and the air so crisp and dry that although we had a few small deck leaks and an occasional dash of spray down the hatch, the cabin was rarely damp; tiny stalactites of salt formed at the deck leaks, and often we used a dustpan and brush to remove the salt crystals from the cabin floor.

Keeping to our plan, we remained well out in the middle of the sea, and the only faint glimpses we got of the mountains were at dawn and dusk, when the persistent haze thinned temporarily. But once we did have a closer look when we approached the shore near Port Berenice, with the idea of resting at an off-lying island if we could find an anchorage there. But night fell before we could make it, so we put about and stood out to sea again.

The disadvantage of keeping out in the middle was that our tacks repeatedly crossed and recrossed the shipping lane, which we found did not follow the neat dotted line on the chart, but was anything up to 25 miles in width. We therefore had to keep a good look-out, one or other of us sticking a head out into the wind and spray every ten minutes day and night. We tried to arrange matters so that we did not have to cross the lane by night, but often that plan was thwarted by a shift of wind making the other the more favourable tack.

Apart from tankers, which today comprise a large proportion of the Red Sea traffic, and by holding relentlessly to collision courses forced us to go about, we had little trouble with shipping, most of which kept a good look-out and behaved correctly and courteously. But I had plenty of excitement one night when I was on watch as we came up with Daedalus Reef, an isolated danger on the shipping lane. Neither *Pilot* nor chart gives any idea of the extent of that reef, on which stands one of the few Red Sea lighthouses. Although I thought *Wanderer* might be able to weather it, I dared not take the risk in case the reef extended out that side, so I took the helm and bore away to pass to leeward of it. Most of the ships in the neighbourhood seemed to be converging on the reef at the same time as ourselves. There were six coming south, all heading as we were to pass west of the reef, and I planned to keep to windward of them, that is, pass between them and the reef. Three other ships, north-bound, appeared to be going to pass outside everyone else. But to my consternation one of these, a fast passenger liner, suddenly altered course to pass inside all the other ships, just where I was aiming to go myself. Obviously she had not seen our stern light, so with a dry feeling in my mouth, I hurriedly put about and headed fast towards the reef, wondering which was the greatest hazard, the reef or the ship. The moonlight was brilliant, and as she swept by that fast ship looked lovely, her shapely hull gleaming, a white bone in her mouth, and I thought of her passengers hidden away in the honeycomb of cabins oblivious of the beauties and excitements of this superlative night. As soon as she was clear I put about again, and a few minutes later one of the south-bound ships, a Union Castle liner, altered course and sliced in between *Wanderer* and the reef, which I then realized could not be as extensive as I had imagined. The night was full of life and interest, nevertheless I was glad when we had worked across the lane and pairs of well-opened masthead lights were passing safely to the eastward.

During our fourteenth night at sea we sighted the high mass of Shadwan Island in the Straits of Gûbal, and soon after dawn we were sailing past its brown and barren slopes, where the only sign of life was the lighthouse. In the straits there are many reefs and about a dozen small islands, and one of the latter, Tawila, has a natural, well-sheltered harbour. With the Red Sea at last safely astern of us, and having made forty-three tacks since leaving Port Sudan, we felt we had earned a rest, so we made our way by eye in among the protecting reefs, and anchored in the harbour on a clay bottom, sheltered from any wind that might blow.

Featureless Tawila, 5 miles by 3, is composed entirely of sand and coral, and nowhere is it more than 45 ft. high. No vegetation grows there, and never have we seen anything more barren; but beneath the cloudless blue sky, with the hazy mainland mountains as background, its rich golden colour was lovely. The wind, which had been so relentless while we were at sea, dropped light soon after our arrival, and the weather was perfect with crisp days and cool, dry nights. Tawila is uninhabited, but now and then fishermen in open feluccas put in ostensibly to catch bait along the shore or scrub the bottoms of their boats, but we believe the real reason was to trans-ship dope, in which there is a considerable traffic from the Sinai Peninsula to Egypt. They looked a tough gang of ruffians, and we did not feel entirely happy at having to share an anchorage with them by night, some of the feluccas having as many as seven men on board. They begged from us, and we gave them cigarettes, but did not let them come on board. We had plenty of water for drinking purposes, but Susan, with a big washing day in mind, tried by signs to ask one of the Arabs who had come off to us in a canoe whether there was any water on Tawila. He went away and returned presently with 4 gallons of very rusty water in an old paraffin tin. This we accepted in return for some sugar, and naturally we supposed he had fetched it from the island; but later, after we had explored the island thoroughly and found no sign of water there, we realized that this was a gift, part of the felucca's own precious supply.

While we were lying there *D'Vara* with the Bradfields aboard came in. They had left Port Sudan a week after us and had experienced quite different weather. Such little wind as they had was mostly fair, and they motored for 111 hours, that is, for almost the whole way. At Aden, Blue had been of the opinion that Tom Steele and I were magnifying the difficulties of the Red Sea; now he is certain of it.

After eight days spent busily and pleasantly at Tawila Island, doing some writing, photography, and maintenance, and stretching our legs on the barren flats of the island, we felt ready to attempt the final 170 miles of windward work up the Gulf of Suez, which is much narrower than the Red Sea, being in places only 10 miles across. The reefs on either side do not run far seaward, but we could expect to find the shipping more concentrated. The first night we spent at Marsa Zeitiya, a deserted bay on the western shore only 25 miles from Tawila; and the following morning, to our surprise and delight, we picked up a fair wind and hurried north at a good 6 knots. This was amazing good fortune in an area where north-west winds prevail throughout the year. By mid-afternoon, however, the weather looked unhealthy; visibility was much reduced, the sky had a yellow tinge, and the wind, after shifting several times from south-east to south-west and back again, settled down to blow fresh from the latter direction. By nightfall we realized that we were about to experience a sandstorm, though not, we hoped, the dreaded *khamsin*, in which visibility is reduced to a few yards, for these do not generally occur until a little later in the year, and to avoid them was one of the reasons we were making the passage north in January.

After dark the wind veered and strengthened, and we were soon plunging heavily in a vicious head-sea, close-hauled in a near gale and unable to steer the course. For us the night was heavy with anxiety. It was absolutely black, except where the beams from our navigation lamps were reflected on the swirling powdery sand ahead and astern, as though we were sailing through thick fog. Several times we sighted the blurred glow of ships' masthead lights; always they were high above us, and therefore uncomfortably close. But that night the ships we met all appeared to be going slowly, and we were able to take any necessary avoiding action in sufficient time, though it was an anxious business. It was difficult to judge, but I believe the visibility could not have exceeded a quarter of a mile, and at times appeared to be only a few yards. Even under much reduced sail *Wanderer* was hard pressed; water, bitterly cold to one's bare feet (we had only one pair of seaboots left), sluiced in the lee side of the cockpit well, and during the short rests we each took below we shivered in our bunks, although we kept on all our clothes under the blankets. Ignorantly we had both supposed the gulf to be a hot place.

In the morning the wind took off, but visibility remained poor, and several hours after rising the sun was only a faint, silvery blur. A film of sand and fine dust lay everywhere in the cabin and had even entered the chronometer box, and sails and rigging above the point reached by spray were coated. Ropes did not render easily through the blocks, the slides of the mainsail stuck in the track when we unrolled the reefs, and our noses and throats felt so congested that we might have been suffering from severe colds.

Uncertain of our position, and unable to find it by observations, for both sun and horizon were too indistinct, we cautiously closed with the western shore at a point where, if our dead reckoning was no more than 5 miles out in either direction, there would be no off-lying dangers. At about noon the peaks of the mountains, which thereabout rise to between 2,000 and

4,000 ft., showed outlined against the pale blue sky; we were able to identify two of them from a sketch in the *Pilot*, and fix our position, which showed that Suez lay 50 miles ahead. We arrived there the following morning with the United Arab Republic flag flying at the starboard crosstree, as the old green and white Egyptian flag is no longer used. In Suez Bay we found thirty-five ships at anchor awaiting transit of the canal, for the sandstorm had caused the port to be closed and the canal convoy system to become disorganized. We made our number at the pilot cutter, and then went on to anchor off the monument at the entrance of the canal. We felt relief that this difficult stage of our voyage was finished, for it had been a struggle and sometimes a worry, but, of course, it could well have been a lot worse.

Having heard that Egypt is a difficult country for a visiting yacht, and that the formalities and paper work in connexion with a transit of the canal are formidable, we had in advance engaged the services of shipping agents—the first time that we had done so, although in the past some had, unasked, kindly given us assistance. The British firm of Messrs. Hull, Blyth & Co. did every possible thing to smooth our transit, and looked after us with fatherly care at both ends of the canal and refused to make any charge.

There are one north-bound and two south-bound convoys each day. A yacht starts her transit at the tail end of a convoy, normally taking two days and stopping for a night at Ismailia on Lake Timsah, about half-way through, for even if she could maintain convoy speed ($7\frac{1}{2}$ knots) she would be unable to carry the huge searchlight which is compulsory for night movement in the canal. But as the convoys were still running late when we left Suez, we had to make two stops instead of one, the first being at El Kabret, where the Great and Little Bitter Lakes merge, and the second at Ismailia. That, incidentally, was the place at which we had planned to stay for a month or more to allow the worst part of the winter to pass before we emerged into the Mediterranean, for the anchorage there is clean and safe and the place is quiet. I had in advance asked for permission to do this, and so had our agents; but permission was refused, and I was advised that the only places at which we might linger were Suez or Port Said.

We had looked forward to the transit with some misgivings, for we had heard frightening stories of the awful things that could happen to little ships when meeting big ones in the canal. It was during the morning of the second day that we met our first south-bound convoy, and this was the moment Susan and I had been dreading. The leading ship, a big Frenchman, appeared to be pushing a considerable amount of water ahead of herself, and seemed from a distance almost to fill the canal. We edged in towards the western bank, steering inside the small buoys which mark the edge of the deep channel. Up we rose on the advancing wave, reaching its summit just before the ship's great flaring bow came abeam, then sank gently into the trough which followed, where the water was sucked away from the canal's steep bank. A breaker followed the trough along the shore, and then came the quarter-wave to lift us up again, but not so high as the bow-wave had done. There appeared to be no tendency for *Wanderer* to be sucked or slewed in any direction, and within a few moments the high steel wall of the ship had slid harmlessly past, and our attention was directed to the next ship of the convoy, a huge Dutch tanker flying light. The disturbance she made was even more alarming as we saw it approaching, but it proved to be no more difficult to negotiate than had been that of the Frenchman, and as she slid past a voice from high up on her bridge hailed us: 'Good luck! Be careful.' A tanker of that size when going the other way laden can pay as much as £11,000 in canal dues. Ship after ship— different shapes and sizes, different colour schemes, different flags—went by in procession at five-minute intervals, and the last to go was President Nasser's graceful steam yacht—there are some advantages in being a dictator.

PLATE 29
Mandraki Harbour, Rhodes, and the ancient mole on which once stood the Colossus. During *sciroccos* great seas thundered against the mole, causing a heavy surge in the harbour.

No dues are charged for small vessels using the canal, and although pilotage is compulsory—one pilot goes only as far as Ismailia, another one taking over there for the run to Port Said—no charge is made for that. Both our pilots were Egyptian; they spoke little English, but seemed to know their business. Although the 87-mile canal cuts for most of its length through flat, desert country, we found much to interest us: ships, dredgers, signal stations, the one and only swing bridge, and even some fishing dinghies and up-river racing fours. For much of the way we had a breeze well forward of the beam, and were able to keep our sails full to assist the motor.

Having arrived safely at busy Port Said, we paid a fantastic bribe to a watchman and left the ship to go to Cairo for a few days, as Frank and Roberta Fuqua, a delightful American couple who had read about our voyage, kindly invited us to stay with them in their apartment on the twenty-first floor of the only skyscraper in the city. They insisted on giving up to us their own bedroom, which had two windows; from one of these we could look down upon the Nile close beneath, where feluccas sailed, and from the other out over the tight-packed roof-tops of the city, sharp cubes of brown and yellow—the kind of view one could not otherwise obtain except from an aeroplane—and at sunrise that view was filled with mystery, for then only the tops of the taller buildings emerged like islands above the smoke and early-morning haze. From the living-room balcony we looked out across the Nile direct at the pyramids, to which our hosts kindly took us among other local places of interest; we also got some small idea of the mental uneasiness which must always be associated with life in a police state. It is interludes such as our visit to Cairo which repay so handsomely the discomforts and anxieties of small-boat voyaging, and that remain so clearly in mind after the latter have fallen into their correct

PLATE 30
Top: A gateway to the old, walled town of Rhodes, which is that rare thing an ancient monument in full daily use. *Bottom:* In the cool silence of the early morning we visited the acropolis of Lindos, which is sited within the battlements of a Crusader castle.

perspective, and they leave one with a feeling of warm gratitude.

On returning to Port Said we found the weather cold, wet, and blowy and the official restrictions too irksome to be tolerated; so we sailed away out into the Mediterranean earlier than we had intended, and three days later came to Limassol on the south coast of Cyprus, having had no wind to start or finish with, and a lot too much in the middle. It was good to be once again in the hospitable hands of the army, but as Cyprus does not offer a small yacht an entirely safe winter berth, we remained for only six pleasant days, and then sailed on in shocking weather to Rhodes, there to remain until mid-April, when the Mediterranean is said to become a more reasonable proposition for small craft.

13

The Mediterranean, and Home

Our berth at Rhodes was a picturesque and entertaining one. We lay in Mandraki Harbour, the entrance to which is guarded by two slender stone columns bearing the red and green harbour lights and crowned by delicate bronze deer, and with anchors out in their direction and stern-lines to the quay, moored Mediterranean fashion. To starboard was the ancient mole on which once stood the Colossus, with three old disused windmills on it and a fort at its end. The busy main street was close to port, and at the far side of it sprawled the big, white market—our convenient shopping centre—with a row of cafés at its seaward side. Above some neighbouring trees towered the battlements of the castle, which together with a maze of narrow streets lies within the moat and the walls of the old town; there we spent a lot of time getting lost and discovering fresh surprises, for the town is that rare thing, an ancient monument in full daily use.

Twice we experienced *sciroccos* (south-east gales) which exceeded 80 knots, the worst, they said, for twenty years; then great seas thundered against the mole, and sent a heavy surge into the harbour. The mess those gales made on board was astonishing, and although we closed the ports and hatches, the cabin was enveloped in dust just as it had been in the Gulf of Suez sandstorm. But there was more than dust on deck; gravel and shingle was carried aboard by the terrific wind, and as the air was filled with spray, our poor ship soon looked as though she had been plastered with cement, and this reached right to the top of the mast.

THE MEDITERRANEAN

We were glad to see *Adios* arrive in the harbour before we left, as we had had no news of her since leaving Aden, but Tom and Janet had a very bad time making Rhodes. They arrived in a strong gale, before which they had run with a sea-anchor towing astern, with sails torn and motor out of action; wisely they did not attempt to make the harbour in such conditions, but sought a berth off the lee side of the island. There they lost both their anchors, were taken in tow by a coaster, and had their bowsprit broken in the process. However, with great perseverance and the help of a skin-diver, Tom eventually recovered the bower anchor and chain, and when we left them he and Janet were planning a cruise through the Grecian archipelago and a winter in Spain. We had news that Blue and Dot Bradfield in *D'Vara* had found a safe berth and a temporary job in Cyprus.

Other cruising friends of ours, Fred and Joan Georgeson from California, in their 11-ton cutter *Alano*, were at the time wintering at Palma de Mallorca, and had made arrangements with the Commodore of the club for *Wanderer* to go on the slip there provided she arrived before 7 June. We were keen to avail ourselves of this opportunity, as our copper sheathing had become oxidized and had lost most of its antifouling properties, and we wanted to give it a coat of antifouling paint to ensure that it remained clean for the homeward trip, part of which would be a beat against the Portuguese trade wind; we also wished to paint the topsides, which had been scarred during our stay in Egypt.

With this date to keep, we felt it would not be possible to cruise through the Greek islands or see anything of Italy, for we knew we could not rely on a fair wind, or perhaps on any wind at all at times, and we remembered the experience of Major Tilman in the ex-pilot cutter *Mischief* at about the same time of year; it took him a month to sail from Port Said to Malta with light winds, and another month for the trip on to Gibraltar with an excess of strong headwinds. We decided, therefore, to go down to Crete, as we particularly wanted to see the Palace of Knossos; then sail direct to Malta, and stop thereafter at Sicily or Sardinia if we had time to spare. We realized that this was not a very ambitious programme, but it might yet turn into a race against time, and after all we were now homeward bound with a desire to see England in early August.

On leaving Mandraki Harbour we stopped for four delightful days in the natural harbour of Lindos, which lies on the south-east side of the island of Rhodes. Close beside us lay the village, its cobbled streets—so twisting, steep, and narrow that donkeys are the only possible means of transport—and its colour-washed houses clustering round a 400-ft. rock on which stands the acropolis, remarkably sited within the battlements of a fine Crusader castle. Because of its setting this is said to be one of the most spectacular sights in the whole of Greece, and it certainly is most impressive when seen, as we saw it, in the cool silence of the early morning before the daily invasion of tourists reached it. In imagination we pictured it thronged with the people who so many centuries ago had climbed those flights of wide stone steps to worship and make sacrifices to their gods in the pillared temples. On one side we looked down to *Wanderer*'s anchorage, and on the other down past the theatre, hewn out of natural rock, into Holy Apostle Harbour, where, according to tradition, St. Paul landed.

We motored away in a calm towards the island of Scarpanto, but the calm was soon replaced by a north-west gale, and for two days we sheltered in a bay off the island's lee side out of touch with the shore, taking turns at reading Cottrell's *The Bull of Minos*, while the wind screamed in the rigging and the anchor dug deeper and deeper into the excellent clay holding ground. Another calm followed the gale, and we motored across Kaso Strait—where William Robinson in *Svaap* beat to windward for a whole week and failed to get through during his circumnavigation—and came to an anchorage in a tiny cove close under the great lighthouse on Cape Sidero, the eastern tip of Crete. The only inhabitants of this barren spot are the lighthouse-keepers and their wives, and although we could speak no word of one another's language, they were friendly and showed us over the oil-fired, hand-wound light.

We then cruised along the north coast of Crete, 130 miles of it, mostly beating against a strong headwind and a rough sea, and we stopped at several places, the most noteworthy being Iraklion, from which town the Palace of Knossos is only a short bus ride. We intended to stay for two days only, but within a few minutes of berthing Susan injured her back so severely that she could not move for several days, and two weeks passed before she was fit enough to go to sea again.

When she was sufficiently recovered to hobble about on my arm, we made the trip to Knossos, and as is our custom, did that early in the day, so that, as at Lindos, we had the place to ourselves. This expedition alone would have made our Mediterranean cruise worth while. The famous archaeologist Sir Arthur Evans, who unearthed the palace, which dates back to about 3000 B.C., rebuilt at his own expense certain parts of it so that people like myself, to whom a pile of stone ruins means very little, can understand what sort of a place it was with its pillared porticoes, its five-flight stairway, its throne-room containing the oldest throne in Europe still in its original position, its treasure vaults, the private apartments of the kings and queens, with their bathrooms, w.c.s, and plumbing. We could imagine it alive with the gay, artistic Minoans with their incredibly small waists—a remarkable feature of both men and women—all those many years ago. The paintings, carvings, and frescoes found there are now in the museum at Iraklion, but excellent reproductions replace them in the palace—of particular note are the 'cup-bearer' and 'priest-king' frescoes—and everything glows with the rich colours of the originals in a green and peaceful countryside. Twice we made the pilgrimage to that exquisite place, and our expectations were generously fulfilled.

We made one more stop in Crete, at Khania, the decaying capital, where we were pestered by ill-mannered but well-dressed little girls long after their supposed bedtime, and then made the trip to Malta direct. With no wind to start with, variable breezes in the middle, and a fair wind to finish up with, the 470-mile trip took five and a quarter days.

One evening a party of four swallows who appeared to need

a rest or a free passage tried to board us. Again and again they attempted to land on the seams of the mainsail, but could find no foothold on the slippery terylene, and unfortunately one of them fell into the sea and was lost. The others then gave up that idea, and after a good deal of experiment and chatter, managed to settle, one of them on the port lower crosstree, one on the fore coachroof in the lee of a ventilator box, and the third on the runner lever within a few inches of the helmsman; so they spent the night with their little heads buried in their feathers. They seemed quite unafraid, and took not the slightest notice of us. Having no insects aboard, we could not feed them, and in view of their positions we had to remain on the same gybe, which put us some miles off course, until they had left us in the morning. We hoped that the 50 miles of westing we gave them that night did not seriously interfere with their navigation.

On arrival at Malta we were treated almost as V.I.P.s, much to our astonishment, for visiting yachts are not unusual there. John Miles, the United States Consul-General—the tallest man we have ever met—unfurled on the balcony of his house his largest flag when he saw *Wanderer* approaching, and he and his wife gave us baths and meals and a specially iced birthday cake for Susan, and lent us a chauffeur-driven car so that we could see something of the island. Everyone else we met did all they could to make our short stay a pleasant one. H.E. the Governor and Lady Grantham kindly had us to lunch, and H.E., who came in person to collect us, insisted on our dinghy oars and rowlocks going along to the palace as well to avoid any risk of theft.

I doubt whether the casual visitor to the George Cross island would see much evidence of the heroic part it played in the war, for many fine new buildings of the same local, warm-coloured stone, and in perfect keeping with the old ones, have filled the gaps and covered the scars, and we gained the impression that the island is a clean, bright, and comparatively

PLATE 31
Wanderer came to an anchorage in a tiny cove at barren Cape Sidero, the eastern tip of Crete.

cheerful place, though the closure of the dockyard has been a severe blow.

All too soon our time at Malta was up, and we were indeed sorry to sail away and leave our new-made friends, and sorrier still when we got out into the Malta Channel and found a fresh headwind blowing. This decided us to make for a port at the west end of Sicily, but by the time we had worked our way to within sight of it, the wind had shifted to the east, and we did not hesitate for a moment in making a change of plan to use that fair wind, for our time was getting short; so we altered course for Cagliari, capital of Sardinia, and 330 miles out from Malta groped our way into it in thick fog. This, our only Italian port, was a surprise for us. Knowing no more about it than the brief description in the *Pilot*, we expected a rather primitive community, but found instead a town laid out with smart shops to attract the tourist, and with tall, new blocks of buildings rising on all sides. This was of little interest to us, but penetrating behind the showy façade we discovered the real Cagliari, a warren of steep, narrow alleys flanked by tenements so high and so close together that the sunlight could scarcely penetrate. The interiors of the dwellings, seen through door or window, appeared to be almost in darkness, and strung across each dim canyon were lines of washing hung up hopefully to dry. In spite of their unpromising habitations, the people we met looked clean and cheerful. One disturbed night in the harbour—barking dogs, blaring radios, bawling drunks, shouting fishermen, and roaring engines made it sleepless—was quite enough, and next morning we sailed for the Balearic Islands.

During this passage we encountered two gales. The first was fair and not of long duration, so we were able to keep going through it under reduced sail; but the second blew from forward of the beam and was accompanied by a heavy swell; for that we hove-to. And while we were lying like that the wind did one

PLATE 32
Susan looks at the 'cup-bearer' fresco in the restored west portico of the Palace of Knossos.

of the remarkable shifts to which we were growing accustomed; it dropped for a few minutes, and then blew with almost the same strength as before, but from north-west, a shift of 90 deg. Very soon an even bigger swell was coming from that direction, and we were astonished at its size, for the fetch out of the Gulf of Lyons (admittedly the stormiest part of the Mediterranean) was not great. The motion produced by the cross swell made us feel dizzy, and when the gale stopped as suddenly as it had started, so great was the left-over confusion that for some hours we could make no progress.

However, in spite of this and our other various setbacks, we managed to reach Palma de Mallorca a day before our esti-mated time of arrival, where we were given a berth in front of the vast Club Nautico and a kind welcome by Sr. Coll, the Commodore; the next day, as promised, *Wanderer* was hauled out on the club slip, which was the cleanest we had ever used. Sr. Coll sent along some of the club boatmen to lend us a hand the first day, as he seemed shocked that Susan and I should be thinking of doing the work ourselves, but when we gave them sheets of wet-and-dry glasspaper with which to rub down the paint, they shook their heads and said they were painters not labourers; so after all we had to do the work ourselves, and in three scorching days undercoated and enamelled the topsides; but Mike and Betty Slator from the motor yacht *Trog*, which wore the Eirean ensign, most kindly helped us to antifoul the copper, and after *Wanderer* had been launched, she lay along-side *Trog* in the cosy, crowded yacht harbour while we com-pleted the refit.

The Balearics consist of three major islands—Menorca, Mallorca, and Ibiza—and several small ones, spread over about three degrees of longitude; they form a pleasant cruising ground, for there are many attractive anchorages, the summer weather is good with clear skies, and the people are friendly and under-stand yachts. Including the time taken over the refit, we spent three weeks among them, and our most enjoyable time was spent at Ibiza, the westernmost, and we think the best of the group. Ibiza town, a pile of colour-washed houses climbing steeply from the water's edge to the summit of a hill on which stands the cathedral, is most attractive, and the harbour, into which it seems almost as though the houses are about to tumble, is busy with the comings and goings of gaily-painted coasters. Unfortunately the sewer discharges into the harbour, but that is something to which one just has to become accustomed when visiting Spanish ports.

At Ibiza we had the good fortune to meet Gordon Sellers. In 1956 he sailed with Ian Major across the Atlantic in the 25-ft. sloop *Buttercup*, making the trade-wind passage under squaresail and vane steering gear. Some years later he set out to make the same crossing in his own small yacht *Falken*, but took the Midi Canal route into the Mediterranean and so reached Ibiza. He so fell in love with that island that his voyage terminated there, and he bought a small farm, but still sails. He took us for a tour of the sun-drenched island (even mounting the steep hill to the cathedral) in his scarlet 1925 model T Ford, which had a geranium behind its ear, and the following day sailed in company with us across to the small island of Española, where we anchored near one another in a bay on the south-west side. After lunch Susan and I swam across to *Falken*, where we sat on deck in the sunshine drinking iced white wine, and when we plunged in for the return swim, Gordon came with us, wearing a wide-brimmed straw hat and a pair of pale yellow shorts, and he was smoking a cigarette. He was still smoking when we reached *Wanderer*, and there we had more wine. We can think of few more pleasant ways of spending a hot afternoon, and this, presumably, is what people mean when they speak of the pleasures of Mediterranean yachting, for with either a lot too much wind or not enough, and frequently with a tiresome, steep swell, we did not find more than five days of enjoyable sailing in the whole 2,500 miles of that long sea. Next morning the two yachts parted, *Falken* to return to Ibiza, *Wanderer* to make one last stop on Ibiza's west coast at the pretty little cove of Cala Badella, where she brought up close to the beach on a sandy bottom with only a few inches under her keel. To reach that place we had passed inside Vedra, a

1,250-ft. island of remarkable architecture; its mountain spires reminded us nostalgically of those of our beloved Moorea, Tahiti's sister island, but there were no guitars, no grass-skirted dancing girls, for Vedra is not inhabited.

The trip across to the Spanish coast was almost windless, but on nearing it we picked up a fresh south-east breeze. This was too good to be wasted, so instead of stopping at Alicante, as had been our original intention, we sailed on through the night and next afternoon came to Cartagena, the only natural harbour on the south-east coast of Spain. An oil refinery has been established in a bay just outside the harbour, and when we left before dawn next day we found the whole harbour covered with oil, our newly painted sides and our mooring-lines were coated with the thick tarry mess, and our deck and rigging with oily soot from a neighbouring man-of-war; we had to go 4 miles to sea before we could draw a bucketful of clean water with which to mix detergent and start the big clean-up.

The trip on to Gibraltar was uneventful. There was not much wind and usually a teasing swell on the quarter to throw us about, and we stopped at two ports only, the ore-loading harbour of Almeria for petrol, and the large, clean, and empty harbour of Motril for a good night's sleep. Not until the exciting, light-spangled silhouette of the Rock of Gibraltar was in sight did we get a worthwhile breeze, and that quickly freshened. The morning weather report from Gibraltar spoke of a 60-knot wind, but fortunately it was not as strong as that, though a full gale was blowing as we rounded Europa Point and made our way to the marina at Waterport, which lies between the northern end of the naval harbour and the air strip

There we lay alongside the immaculate 11-ton cutter *Alano* with our friends Fred and Joan Georgeson and their crew Edward Shute aboard. Without these friends to talk to and do things with we would have found Gibraltar a very dull place, for we met no one else except the manager of the marina, who is a busy man, and the Assistant Queen's Harbourmaster, who called only to inspect our Admiralty warrant to fly the blue ensign. No doubt this was very good for us after our V.I.P. treat-ment at Malta, which perhaps had gone to our heads, and the apes high up on the Rock put us in proper perspective, for they judge their visitors purely on their banana-carrying capacity.

Alano was bound for England, and the evening before her departure we had Fred, Joan, and Edward aboard for dinner. After the meal we played some of the tape-recordings we had made of island music in the South Pacific. These were so popular that we had to play them over and over again.

Next morning Fred hailed us. 'We've changed our minds,' he said.

'Whatever do you mean?' I asked.

'We're not going to England after all,' he replied. 'We're turning left instead of right when we get out of here, bound for the West Indies and Tahiti. Your Pacific island music has sure taken our fancy.'

We left the marina in company with them, but instead of slipping out through the Strait of Gibraltar, we put into the Spanish port of Algeciras only 4 miles across the bay, for in preparation for the 1,200-mile passage home we wanted to swing and make out new deviation cards for the compass and radio direction-finding set. We did what was necessary there in complete calm and considerable heat, nauseated at times by the stink of sewage which permeated the harbour, and were glad to leave and motor 5 miles down the coast to the eastern entrance of the strait, where we found a strong west wind funnelling through. We reefed the mainsail, changed to the small staysail, and tried to beat through, but after making one tack out into the middle, where the sea was rough, and another back to the northern shore, we found we had lost ground, so we gave up and headed back for Algeciras. As soon as we had shut out the strait we lost the wind, and in sweltering heat motored to our anchorage.

The narrowest part of the strait is 8 miles wide and about 10 miles long from Carnero Point at the east end and Tarifa light at the west end. To compensate for the incessant loss by evapora-tion in the Mediterranean, an east-going current nearly always runs through the strait. There are also tidal streams, but when the west-going stream is running its effect in the middle of the strait is only to weaken the east-going current, not to overcome it. A strong and continued west wind is said to raise the level of the sea outside and thus increase the strength of the current. Near the shores, however, the west-going tidal stream does overcome the current, but to take advantage of this one needs to be very close to the coast, off which there lie rocks, among them La Perla, which has a depth of 1¼ fathoms over it; unfortunately there is a wreck on this rock which is said to show at low water. This danger lies less than a mile from the shore, and is unmarked, yet to gain the advantage of the fair tidal stream one has to pass inside it. This at first we were not prepared to do with a strong headwind.

During the following eight days, always timing our arrival to coincide with the start of the west-going tide, we made five more attempts to get through the strait, and as we became more desperate we even tried to pass inside La Perla. But on every occasion the relentless west wind blew at near gale strength, and we failed to make any headway against it, the steep sea which it raised, and the current. We tried by day and we tried by night; we tried under sail, we tried motor-sailing, and we even tried under motor alone; but we could make no progress. It was particularly irritating after each abortive attempt to go back into the area of almost permanent calm north of Carnero Point, and to have to motor to our anchorage. After several days we abandoned Algeciras in favour of Getares Bay, which lies a little closer to the strait. There it was cooler, the water was clean, and we could bathe; but in using an open anchorage on the Spanish coast anywhere near Gibraltar there is some risk of being fired on by the *guardia civil*, who naturally enough are jumpy about smuggling, for this is done in a big way by so-called yachts, mostly power vessels wearing the British flag and manned by foreigners.

It was some small comfort to read in Beecher's *Winds and Currents of the Mediterranean* that in the days of sail it was not uncommon for a hundred ships to be seen at anchor off

Algeciras waiting for a fair wind to take them through the strait. But they, no doubt, were square rigged, and hitherto we had regarded our own ship as a reasonably efficient fore-and-after.

On the eleventh day after leaving Gibraltar we again motored in the usual calm down to the strait, the seventh time we had done so, and to our joy on rounding Carnero Point found that the west wind had died. Under power we hugged the northern shore, passed inside La Perla, skirted the rocks off the next headland, and finding the inshore stream fair and fast, swept past Tarifa lighthouse at 9 a.m. How thankful we were to see that white tower slip astern, for it had been our goal for many days; but even then we were not through the strait, which continues for another 25 miles to Cape Trafalgar; however, after Tarifa it widens so that the current is not so strong and the wind does not funnel through with such violence as in the narrows.

It was good to be once more out in the familiar North Atlantic, but the wind was now so light that three and a half days passed before we rounded Cape St. Vincent. There we crossed our outward track at the point where we had been on the evening of 6 September 1959, when outward bound for the coast of Morocco. For the second time in her ten years of life little *Wanderer* had, by heading month after month towards the west horizon, made a circumnavigation of the globe, and we had a feeling of great affection for her. Although we could not experience complete satisfaction until such time as we reached the port from which we had set out, clearly this was the occasion for a little celebration. We still had a Dundee cake on board and a *garafon* of Spanish white wine, and as I sat in the cockpit in the sunshine with the shapely bottle under my arm, I felt as Omar Khayyám must have felt, for there was Thou in the hatchway munching cake and passing up slice after slice in exchange for glass after glass of wine.

At that point we felt the first breath of the Portuguese trade wind, the fresh northerly that throughout the summer blows with great constancy down the west coasts of Spain and Portugal, and is accompanied by a current with a rate of from $\frac{1}{2}$ to 1 knot. The recommended procedure for a north-bound sailing vessel encountering this wind is to stand offshore on the starboard tack until she falls in with a slant to take her to the English Channel. That is what we did, but with the exception of two days we had a headwind until we reached the latitude of Ushant. I believe the reason for this was that we never got sufficiently far to the north-west, as we were unable to resist the temptation to steer the direct course during those two days of fair wind. However, that part of the passage was by no means as unpleasant as we had expected it might be. The weather was fine, though we found it chilly, and had to put more blankets on our bunks and fetch out all our winter clothes; the nights grew shorter as we made northing, while the wind was rarely fresh and was more often moderate in strength. Although at times there was a jump of sea, not often was there much swell, and most of the way the ship steered herself. As we were well outside the shipping lane, we were able to have most of each night in our bunks, with the riding light burning brightly on the weather runner, but after passing Finisterre we met many tunnymen, and had to keep a proper look-out.

And so we slowly worked our way up to the latitude of Ushant, where with a falling glass the wind shifted to the south-west and blew with gale force for a few hours. At the time we were on the edge of the Continental shelf, and although the sea was of no great height it was rough and confused, so we hove-to for six hours. As usual on those occasions, which seemed to us to have occurred too often during the past six months, we chocked ourselves off in our bunks, dozing, reading, and listening to the noise aloft; a little apprehensive, though with no good reason to worry. Twice we smelt the sickly-sweet stench of oil, and in the evening when the wind moderated and I looked out, I found the whole ship, cockpit, deck, sides, rigging, and the sail up as far as spray could reach, spattered with gobs and streaked with smears of thick brown oil emulsified with water. Obviously some tanker to windward of us had pumped the sludge out of her tanks, and the driving spray had carried this disgusting filth all over us. So slippery was the deck that

we could not safely make our way about it without first removing the oil, and that job took us several hours of nauseating
work with rolls of toilet tissue and paraffin. The motion was
violent, and as we worked on hands and knees bursts of spray
soaked us repeatedly, for our oilskins had long since been ren-
dered useless by tropical conditions.

Then we made sail, and two evenings later, having been
headed off, we made our landfall on the brilliant flashing light
of the Lizard. The sunset was lurid; a bar of angry crimson lay
along the horizon below a sky heavy with rolling black cloud,
which momentarily reflected the light as the sun dipped; again
the glass was falling.

By midnight the wind had backed to the south-east and the
loom of the distant lights at Falmouth disappeared in rain. The
wind continued to freshen and it seemed we were about to have
another hard blow, a conclusion which was confirmed by the
morning forecast. Close-hauled, the motion was growing violent,
so we hove-to for breakfast and to change our wet clothes. By
the time the meal had been cooked, eaten, and cleared away,
the wind had backed to north and freshened to a force 8 gale.
We remained hove-to on the inshore tack.

It was August Bank Holiday, and a memorable one when
there were gale warnings for many areas, and several lifeboats
put out from their stations, while farther north a Scottish fishing
vessel had foundered and thirty ships were searching for the
survivors. By account we were ten miles south of the Eddystone,
that is, in the shipping lane between Lizard and Start, and this
was confirmed by the ships which from time to time loomed out
of the murk to east and west. Heavy rain continued most of the
day and reduced visibility to a mile or less, while the wind
slowly backed to north-west. For the present there was nothing
we could do but keep as good a lookout as possible.

In the evening the rain stopped, and there, clear-cut against
the background of Devonshire hills, stood the thin, grey pencil
of the Eddystone lighthouse only a few miles away. The wind
by then had moderated a little, and as there was no future in
remaining hove-to and slowly fore-reaching towards the shore,

for the forecast promised more gales to come, we bore away for the Start and the run up Channel.

Night was falling as we hurried past Bolt Head, black and sinister, and as we passed the Salcombe entrance, clear above the noise of wind and sea came the double explosion of the life-boat maroons. A few minutes later, when we had brought the Prawle abeam, I saw what I took to be the lights of the Sal-combe life-boat coming out; they passed astern and vanished seaward in the rain which had started to fall again.

Off the Start the wind resumed gale force, but as it was blowing obliquely off the land the sea was not too heavy, and throughout the night we ran fast on our way to clear Portland Bill by seven miles. The rain continued all night, but it did not much reduce visibility, and as we were just inside the shipping lane we had nothing to worry about. At breakfast time, with the tide against us, we had the Bill bearing north, the wind had dropped a little, and soon dropped more, and at noon when we beat into Studland Bay there was only a gentle breeze, and soon there was a little sunshine to help dry our wet things. We had put in there for a rest and a tidy-up after being at sea for twenty-one days, and we had a wonderfully silent, smooth, and sleep-filled night. The passage home had certainly been a slow one, for we had made good only 1,130 miles in those three weeks.

Next morning, 8 August, we found a moderate west wind with showers and some sunshine as we ran under full sail across Poole Bay towards the Needles. How jolly the English scene looked; the land was green, the sea was green, and all around were yachts, the first we had seen for many a day.

In the early afternoon *Wanderer* entered Yarmouth, her home port, with the ensigns of the seventeen countries she had visited flying in a colourful string from her starboard upper crosstree. News of her approach had, apparently, been sent ahead from the Needles, for some of the yachts in the little harbour were dressed overall and blew their sirens as she entered. Charlie Attrill, the harbourmaster, met us and led us to our berth, where he took our lines and soon we were secure. Everyone was so very kind that our eyes were a little damp.

Wanderer III

Wanderer III is in most respects an orthodox British yacht of heavy-displacement type and with narrow beam. I believe greater beam would have made her more comfortable, and a short, sawn-off counter would have improved her appearance and made the bumkin unnecessary; but we could afford neither.

She was built for Susan and me in 1952 by Messrs. William King Ltd., of Burnham-on-Crouch, Essex, to designs by Messrs. Laurent Giles & Partners Ltd., of Lymington, Hampshire, and she cost £3,300. Both workmanship and materials were faultless, and during the building there was never a cross word between us.

Her dimensions are: length over all 30 ft. 3 in.; length on the waterline 26 ft. 5 in.; designed draught 5 ft.; but throughout the voyage she was drawing about 9 in. more than that because of her rather heavy construction, and the weight of food, water, and other things she had on board. Her Thames tonnage is 8, and her displacement in seagoing trim about 9 tons.

Keel and deadwood are of elm. The ballast keel, about 3 tons, is of lead, and there is no inside ballast. Stem, sternpost, frames, carlines, and deck beams are of English oak. All the frames are steam bent and some are doubled; a few of the floors are of oak, but most are of wrought iron. Keel bolts and chainplate bolts are of steel, but all other fastenings are of copper, bronze, or brass. Planking is of iroko, a West African timber similar to teak, and is finished $1\frac{1}{8}$ in. thick. Coamings, cockpit, hatches, rail, and cabin sole are also of iroko. Decks are of tongued-and-grooved western red cedar covered with canvas and painted. The bottom is copper sheathed.

The internal joinery work is of light African 'mahogany', varnished up to sideboard level and painted white above. At the after end of the accommodation a large galley with stainless-steel-covered bench (there is no sink) and swinging two-burner Para-Fin stove (Primus type) faces the oilskin locker and navigation space, which has a chart table with drawers and shelves below it capable of holding up to 400 Admiralty charts stowed flat, but we find 250 a more convenient number to have aboard at one time. The cabin has a Dunlopillo settee-berth each side of a fixed table with hinged leaves on which high fiddles can be fixed; above the settee backs are shelves for 150 books. The forward ends of the berths extend beneath sideboards to take the sleeper's feet at night and the bedding in the daytime, and canvas bunkboards lie flat beneath the mattresses when not in use. Each side, and forward of the sideboards, are large lockers with shelves for clothes, photographic equipment, medical supplies, typewriter, etc. The forepeak houses a Baby Blake w.c., the chain locker, and four water cans, and has stowage space for all sails, warps, spare rope, and navigation lamps; there is also a work-bench and a large bin for tools and bosun's stores.

Sixty gallons of fresh water are carried in three tanks which can be shut off from one another and filled separately, and the four cans in the forepeak bring the total supply up to 70 gallons, enough for two people for 80 days or more. Provisions for a similar length of time can be carried in the many lockers with which the yacht is provided; each is numbered and a list of the contents made. Ventilation is by six opening ports in the coachroof coamings, four large cowls (the forward two are of the water-trap type), and a mushroom vent at bow and stern. During hot weather in port we spread a terylene awning to shade the deck abaft the mast and sometimes rig a canvas windsail to blow down one of the hatches.

The auxiliary motor is an 8 h.p. Stuart Turner two-stroke running on petrol, and drives a two-blade propeller on the centreline. In a calm and smooth water the maximum speed is 5 knots; 12 gallons of fuel in two tanks right aft give a range of about 80 miles. A belt-driven dynamo charges a 12 volt battery, but electricity is used only for emergency or convenience, and normally we use paraffin, of which 10 gallons are carried in cans in a cockpit locker.

The steering compass was made by Messrs. Henry Browne & Sons, and is of the grid type; the grid is luminous, the north-south line consisting of a thin glass tube filled with luminous powder and sealed, so that the compass fluid shall not dull it. This instrument is installed beneath a pane of unbreakable glass in the bridge deck, where, after correction, it has little deviation, but some heeling error. A hand-bearing compass is shipped in a bracket on the after leg of the cabin table, where it serves as a tell-tale when we are both below at the same time.

Wanderer is rigged as a jib-headed sloop; the maximum sail area, with mainsail and genoa set, is 600 sq. ft. The mast of silver spruce is hollow, but the main boom and spinnaker booms are solid, and all are painted white to keep them as cool as possible in the tropics, and so preserve the glue with which they are held together. The

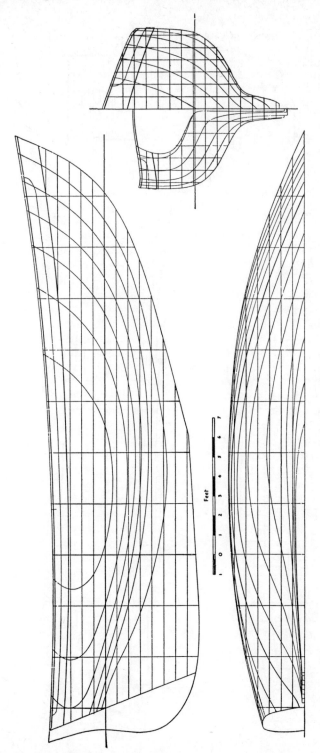

Wanderer III: Lines

Dimensions: L.O.A. 30 ft. 3¼ in.; L.W.L. 26 ft. 4¾ in.; beam 8 ft. 5 in.; draught 5 ft.; Thames measurement 8 tons; displacement 16,000 lb.; lead keel 7,000 lb.

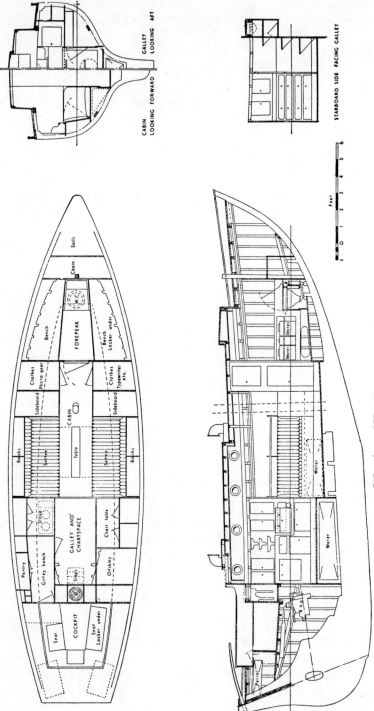

WANDERER III

Mainsail	279 sq. ft.
Genoa	322 sq. ft.
No. I Staysail	144 sq. ft.
No. 2 Staysail	92 sq. ft.
No. 3 Staysail	43 sq. ft.
Trysail	75 sq. ft.
Twin Spinnakers (each)	165 sq. ft.

Feet
1 0 1 2 3 4 5 6

Wanderer III: SAIL PLAN

sails were all made by Messrs. Cranfield & Carter Ltd., of Burnham-on-Crouch. The mainsail is of terylene machine sewn, but each seam has an additional row of hand-made stitches as an insurance against chafe. Worm-type roller reefing gear is fitted, and to facilitate the use of this the lower third of the luff of the sail is not fitted with slides, but with a lacing. The three staysails—referred to in the text as large, small, and storm, the first two being of terylene, the last of flax—are set on the lower forestay; the cotton genoa and the nylon ghoster are set on the topmast stay. There is also a flax trysail of 75 sq. ft., and nylon twin spinnakers for self-steering before the wind of 125 sq. ft. each.

All the standing rigging, except the stainless forestays and bronze rod bumkin bobstays, is of galvanized steel wire, and this we protected with frequent applications of boiled linseed oil; but after 70,000 miles of cruising it is now due for renewal, and we shall probably replace it with stainless wire. All halyards and sheets are of three-strand terylene rope, but the topping lift is of nylon.

Two 35 lb. C.Q.R. anchors are carried and 45 fathoms of $\frac{5}{16}$ in. tested chain, together with $1\frac{1}{8}$ in. nylon springs, which in shallow water we find more effective in preventing snubbing than a weight and traveller. There are two 30 fathom warps, one of hemp and the other of nylon, as well as 20 fathoms of $1\frac{1}{2}$ in. terylene. No windlass is fitted, but a stout pawl mounted over the stemhead roller holds each link of chain as it is hauled in, and in my opinion is superior to a windlass in a vessel of this size.

A 7 ft. 3 in. Viking Marine alloy pram dinghy is carried bottom up on chocks on the coachroof between the mast and the companion-way.

The total cost of the voyage, including food, drink, tobacco, clothes, fuel, charts, and the maintenance of the ship and her gear to a high standard, was £700 a year; but this sum does not include the cost of photographic materials.

APPENDIX 2

Photography and Tape-Recording

We have so often been asked what cameras we use (nobody has yet asked me what typewriter I use) that perhaps a few words about photography and tape-recording, as applied to this voyage, may not be out of place here.

Colour stills

All the colour photographs reproduced in this book, except those from Aden onwards, and Plate 11, were taken with a Contax I, 35 mm. camera about thirty years old. For this we had three interchangeable lenses: a 35 mm. (wide angle) which was used for nearly all shots taken on board; a 50 mm. (normal), and an 85 mm. (long focus). The latter is a useful lens, but is difficult to hold steady, and a short exposure is needed when using it on board. Pictures after leaving Aden were taken with a Canonflex single-lens reflex 35 mm. camera, also with interchangeable lenses; Plate 11 is from four frames cut from the 16 mm. movie film.

As far as Aden we used Kodachrome I film; thereafter we used the new Kodachrome II, and for shots in poor light found this higher-speed film a great advantage, and could detect little difference in colour in the finished transparencies.

Black-and-white stills

We used Kodak Plus-X film for the purpose of illustrating articles sold to *Yachting* and *Yachting World*. For this work we also used a Contax I camera a little older than the other and with the same interchangeable lenses.

Colour movies

When planning to make a movie film of the voyage we had two ideas in mind. One was to produce a film with which to bore our friends and perhaps give public performances; the other was to attempt to enter the television field.

The camera we used was a Bell and Howell 70 DR 16 mm., with

a three-lens turret accommodating a wide-angle, a normal, and a long-focus lens; the action of turning the turret moves the appropriate viewfinder into position automatically. We found this to be an excellent and rugged instrument, and perhaps because it has none of the fancy gadgets which are sometimes considered to be so essential, it served us well and put up with some hard treatment. Ashore whenever possible we used it on a sturdy wooden tripod, and a delayed-action release could be coupled up with the cable release when we both needed to appear in the picture together. Susan acted as continuity girl, keeping a written record of every shot and of the clothes we were wearing.

For television use, or if sound is to be put on a film, the film must be projected, and therefore shot, at 24 frames per second instead of 16 f.p.s., which is the speed used by most amateurs. Besides using more film, this, of course, means that a shorter exposure is given to each frame, and a larger stop has therefore to be used; so we were glad on reaching Aden to be able to change from Kodachrome I, which until then we had been using, to the faster Kodachrome II. In all we exposed about 8,000 ft. (one and a half miles), and of this the B.B.C. televised 2,300 ft. in two half-hour instalments.

Filters and exposure

As Kodachrome exposed on or near the sea tends to be excessively blue, we always used ultra-violet filters to hold back some of the blue light, and each lens was fitted with its own filter kept permanently in position. This also applied to the still cameras, and although the ultra-violet filter has no effect with black-and-white film exposed at normal altitudes, it does protect the lens from spray, dust, and fingerprints, and it can never do any harm. With this type of filter no increase of exposure is needed.

We used a Weston photo-electric exposure meter with both types of film, and did not experience the exposure troubles which have bothered some people working in the tropics.

Protection from damp, and processing

Aboard a small vessel in the tropics humidity is the chief difficulty with which the photographer is likely to be confronted. Cameras and their lenses are liable to be harmed by it, and colour film is particularly susceptible after it has been exposed. We therefore kept all the cameras (and the tape-recorder) in plastic bags together with small cans of silica gel, a desiccating agent which changes colour from blue to pink when saturated. As soon as the silica gel showed signs of changing colour, we heated it up on the hotplate of the galley stove until it turned blue, let it cool in a large tin, and then replaced it. We did not replace exposed films in their containers, but kept them loosely in a sealed tin with silica gel, and as soon as we reached a port which had air communication, sent the colour films to the processing station by airmail.

All the black-and-white films were developed on board as soon after exposure as possible. Microdol developer was used, but temperature control was not possible, and some films were developed at a temperature as high as 87°F., the time being shortened as was found necessary by experiments made before the voyage started. On this trip we did not carry the gear needed for making bromide enlargements, as we did on the first trip. Instead we took more shots of each subject, and sent the duplicate negatives to the editors, who were kind enough to accept them and all the bother they entailed.

Tape-recording

At the time we were preparing for the voyage the only available portable dry-battery-operated tape-recorder with loudspeaker play-back facilities was the Austrian-made Stuzzi. This makes use of four small pocket-torch batteries, on which it will record for 30 hrs. or play back for 60 hrs. We used steel-encased batteries which have a very long shelf life. The speeds of this machine are $1\frac{7}{8}$ and $3\frac{3}{4}$ in. per sec., and better results can be obtained with a speed of $7\frac{1}{2}$ i.p.s. (the B.B.C. uses a speed of 15 i.p.s.).

As novices at recording we made a lot of mistakes, two of the more important being these: We usually forgot to fade in and fade out at the beginning and end of a recording, so that any background noises started and finished too abruptly. The other mistake was that, with an eye to economy, we recorded on both halves of the tape, so that subsequent editing of one recording was not possible without interfering with the other; so it was necessary to copy our recordings on another machine, with some loss of quality. However, our recordings have given us a lot of pleasure, and some of those we made in the South Pacific islands were used as background music with my commentary for the television shows; but I think we ought to do much better in the future.

Table of Times and Distances

	Time on passage in days and hours	Distance in sea miles
19 July to 12 Oct. 1959 Yarmouth, I.W., to St. Vincent, Cape Verdes, via ports in Spain, Portugal, Morocco, and Canaries		2,930
19 Oct. to 7 Nov. St. Vincent to Georgetown, British Guiana	19d. 9h.	2,052
24 Nov. to 5 Jan. 1960 Georgetown to Curaçao via Barbados and Grenadines		1,038
7 Jan. to 13 Jan. Curaçao to Cristobal, Panama Zone	6d. 14h.	718
20 Jan. Transit of canal to Balboa	11h.	40
4 Feb. Balboa to Taboga		10
6 Feb. to 18 Feb. Taboga to Hood I., Galápagos	12d. 4h.	940
19 Feb. to 28 Feb. Amongst the Galápagos Is.		108
29 Feb. to 29 March Charles I. to Mangareva	29d. 2h.	2,893
12 April to 23 April Mangareva to Tahiti	11d. 8h.	889

24 April to 19 June Day sails Tahiti and Moorea		50
20 June to 29 June Moorea to Rarotonga	8d. 23h.	603
16 July to 2 Aug. Rarotonga to Tongatapu, Tonga	16d. 4h.	858
3 Aug. to 29 Aug. Amongst the Tonga Is.		207
30 Aug. to 4 Sept. Vava'u to Suva, Fiji	5d. 5h.	461
5 Sept. to 22 Sept. Amongst the Fiji Is.		60
23 Sept. to 7 Oct. Ono to Russell, New Zealand	14d. 5h.	1,090
8 Oct. to 4 April 1961 In New Zealand waters		650
5 April to 18 April Russell to Nouméa, New Caledonia	13d. 10h.	900
19 April to 4 May In New Caledonian waters		45
5 May to 20 May Ile Ducos to Port Moresby, Papua-New Guinea	15d. 1h.	1,368
6 June to 19 June Port Moresby to Horn I. via Bramble Cay and other anchorages		365
20 June to 7 July Horn I. to Darwin via Arnhemland anchorages		785
18 July to 30 July Darwin to Christmas I.	12d. 6h.	1,512
2 Aug. to 6 Aug. Christmas I. to Keeling Cocos	4d. 2h.	534
1 Sept. to 27 Sept. Keeling Cocos to Mahé, Seychelles	26d. 2h.	2,565
28 Sept. to 5 Oct. Amongst the Seychelles		10

6 Oct. to 31 Oct.
  Mahé to Aden   25d. 10h.   1,419
1 Nov. to 14 Dec.
  In Aden Harbour   8
15 Dec. to 17 Dec.
  Aden to Perim I. via Ras Imran   102
20 Dec. to 28 Dec.
  Perim I. to Port Sudan   7d. 23h.   583
9 Jan. 1962 to 23 Jan.
  Port Sudan to Tawila I.   14d. 4h.   542
1 Feb. to 4 Feb.
  Tawila I. to Suez via Marsa
  Zeitiya   171
6 Feb. to 9 Feb.
  Transit of Suez Canal with stops
  at El Kabret and Ismailia   90
25 Feb. to 12 March
  Port Said to Rhodes via Cyprus   484
15 April to 11 May
  Rhodes to Khania via Lindos,
  Scarpanto, and anchorages in
  Crete   272
13 May to 18 May
  Khania to Malta   5d. 7h.   472
24 May to 29 May
  Malta to Cagliari, Sardinia   4d. 21h.   330
30 May to 3 July
  Cagliari to Gibraltar via
  Balearics and ports in Spain   880
7 July to 16 July
  In Gibraltar Bay and to
  Getares Bay   7
17 July to 7 Aug.
  Getares Bay to Studland Bay   21d. 6h.   1,130
8 August
  Studland Bay to Yarmouth, I.W.   18
                                                              ———
          Total distance made good in sea miles   30,189
          Best day's run   169 sea miles
          Number of places visited   140

Index